Learn to

"SELL"

And

STAY EMPLOYED

In any Economy

About James R. Thompson

"Highest level of sales competency, fullness of integrity, richness of character; these are just a few of the words that describe James. In his sales efforts, he is strategic, knowledgeable and engaging and he plays big.

He has been in the highest echelons.

But there is another side to James that is definitely worth noting: his writing. His books run the full gamut from business support to highly personal. What they all have in common is an amazing heart which he's not afraid to show.

James is one of those unique people that you want to do business with because, in simplest terms: He knows so much."

-Howard Bronson
Author:
'Free Enterprise',
'Dog Gone,
'How to Heal a Broken Heart in 30 Days'
Senior Consultant, The Wildfire Foundation
CEO, The Free Market institute
Creative Director at Brilliant Minds INK

Learn to
"SELL"
And
STAY EMPLOYED
In any Economy

Over One Hundred Proven Sales Techniques
No Matter What Your Field

JAMES R THOMPSON

Visit: learntosellandstayemployed.com

iUniverse, Inc.
New York   Bloomington

Learn to "SELL" and Stay Employed in Any Economy
Over One Hundred Proven Sales Techniques
No Matter What Your Field

iUniverse books may be ordered through booksellers or by contacting:

iUniverse
1663 Liberty Drive
Bloomington, IN 47403
www.iuniverse.com
1-800-Authors (1-800-288-4677)

Because of the dynamic nature of the Internet, any Web addresses or links contained in this book may have changed since publication and may no longer be valid. The views expressed in this work are solely those of the author and do not necessarily reflect the views of the publisher, and the publisher hereby disclaims any responsibility for them.

ISBN: 978-1-4401-4212-3 (pbk)
ISBN: 978-1-4401-4213-0 (ebk)

Printed in the United States of America

iUniverse rev. date: 4/30/2009

Forward

This book is for everyone who wants to succeed in life.

No matter what your career, position in life, or goals you must know how to sell.

Learning to sell, and sell effectively is "the" most universal employment skill.

But what about selling or using" sales techniques" in today's challenging economy?

The stories in this book spanned the mid 1970's through today. During these decades we experienced incredible economic challenges.

The mid-seventies had gas lines.

The early eighties had prime interest rates over twenty percent.

The late eighties had the worst stock market drop in four decades.

The late nineties had the bursting of the technology bubble and the stock market tanked again.

And now, the country is reeling from failing banks, the credit market has dried up, unemployment is reaching monumental levels and people are losing their homes.

Learning the art of persuasion is essential to survival.

If you are out of work, you must learn how to sell yourself.

"Learn to SELL and STAY EMPLOYED" contains true sales stories. My intention is that through them and the techniques presented, you will learn to sell and stay employed or get employed for as long as you want to work.

-James R. Thompson

Chapter 1

"You Love Me!
You Really, Really Love Me!"
-Sally Fields

Always do what you are afraid to do.
- Ralph Waldo Emerson

"Jim, the State Employee Benefits Committee has decided to award you and your firm the contract."

I was driving through a mind-blowing "white-out" of a snow storm when I took the call on my cell phone. All I could think to say when I heard his words was to ask him: "Why?"

"Well," my client responded. "As you know, you represented the smallest and youngest vendor for this forty million dollar contract, and the incumbent has been fighting for a year to keep the business. But it boiled down to a couple of simple things."

"What?" I humbly asked while trying to drive my car through the snow in order to find the long-term airport parking sign.

"You were always available whenever we had a question.

When you didn't know they answer you told us.

And you got back to us with the answer when you found it."

I was dumbfounded. I thought, "Who wouldn't be available when a forty-million dollar prospect had a question?"

Apparently ten other bidders hadn't.

"Thank you." I responded, "This is great news!"

"That's not all." He said. "As you know, I Chair a state-wide purchasing coalition representing several other entities including banks, universities, and utilities and they have asked me to ask you if you would include all of them in the deal according to the same terms." He took a breath and so did I.

"Of course separate contracts would be needed for each individual entity. But they all want the same volume discount."

"I wish I could tell you 'yes'." I said. "But as you know, I have to confer with my CEO on a deal this big. Why don't we conference him in."

We did and My CEO agreed. After all, our newest and largest client was asking for the order. And indeed, he told my CEO why we were chosen: they loved me. They really, really loved me.

The combined contracts were worth well over one hundred million dollars per year and they signed on for multi-year contracts which they all then renewed throughout my tenure with the company.

So this is one of those sales stories where you get the "how I got the sale" at the beginning.

The story that leads to the "how" is one that just came natural to me.

Well, kind of natural.

My parents taught me to be honest and courteous. And that is how I won this account and dozens like it.

When prospects called me I called them back.

When I didn't have an answer I told them so.

When I got an answer I gave it to them right away.

These are pretty simple concepts. But the rest of the story could be the makings of a "Paul Harvey" radio commentary.

This large Western State was required to take all multi-million dollar contracts out to bid every three years. At the time, I was working for a company out of St. Louis where I spent a week a month building and managing a proposal group and the other three weeks working out of my home office in Pennsylvania.

In addition to oversight for several hundred voluminous proposals we cranked out each year, I also had responsibility to go after large accounts.

I was the company's elephant hunter. I reported directly to the CEO and CFO who had originally recruited me to be their Vice President of Sales. I had declined the position, not wanting to relocate permanently to St. Louis. But I worked closely with the four other Vice Presidents of Sales that the company burned out during my nine-year tenure. I also teamed up with most members of the national sales force. Some saw me as a threat. Those that didn't made a crap-load of commissions.

The opportunity to bid on this forty-million dollar State contract came unsolicited. Rather than simply responding to their request for proposal (RFP), I called and asked if I could meet with them. They were surprised and said that the pre-bid conference was open to all bidders and they would be able to answer my questions at that time. I asked them how many other bidders were involved. They told me they had sent RFPs to ten and hoped for responses from all of them. I asked again if they would allow me a private audience so that I could make sure our response to their RFP would work for both of us. They were surprised that I would want to travel all the way from Pennsylvania to Helena, Montana.

I persisted.

They acquiesced.

But they insisted that they didn't want a sales presentation. I told them that I wouldn't even bring a brochure.

They actually thought that was pretty funny.

When I arrived a meeting had been arranged with several people from the Employee Benefits Department to meet with me.

Since I didn't bring a brochure I simply asked them if they would tell me why they were going out to bid. I also asked them to explain why our little company had been chosen out of a potential of forty vendors to provide one of ten bids.

Then I sat back, listened and took notes.

The meeting lasted over two hours. It only ended then because there is only one flight per day in and out of Helena and I had to catch it. During the meeting I tried hard to just probe and listen. But they wore me down and I spilled my guts about how good the little company was that I represented. And for questions that I couldn't answer I called my CEO. I called him from the State's conference room phone, during the meeting! I put him on the speaker and introduced him to everyone. In a sincere self-deprecating way, I let them know that he was the brains behind the entire operation.

It turned out, that he really liked hearing my praises of him, from them.

He returned the favor by touting his trust in me.

They were impressed that he was so accessible.

It was a love fest.

Well, not so much.

Turns out that one of the staff members in the meeting was very tight with the incumbent vendor and had them on the phone and back over to the client's office the next day with a litany of reasons why my company could never handle their business.

But the dialogue continued. I received the list and responded quickly and honestly.

When we were chosen to be one of four finalists I brought in my CEO with me. Turns out he had been born and lived for a few short years in Kalispell just up the highway from Helena, Montana. He knew better than to have told me that before our meeting. Like most sales executives I liked to use everything in my arsenal. But it turns out that a hometown boy wasn't as effective as homespun honesty and courtesy.

So from this one successful sales story are several techniques that never fail no matter what you are selling. I have listed them in order of the sales cycle for this hundred million dollar deal:

1. Unsolicited business should be humanized as soon as possible. Get in front of the buyer(s).

2. Once in front of your buyer(s) try your best to listen to why they are buying. For good salesmen this is very difficult. For great salesmen it is imperative.

3. Introduce up-line management as soon as possible through a positive introduction. If you do not believe in or trust your boss, sell for somebody else. No matter what the product buyers must be given the opportunity to believe that it is you and the company that stand behind your promises.

4. Return their phone calls by the end of the day (their time).

5. If you do not know the answers to their questions, tell them immediately. No hesitation, no vacillation no equivocation.

The way to love anything is to realize that it might be lost.
- G.K. Chesterton, author

CHAPTER 2

The Home Run

My life is my message.
- Mahatma Gandhi

The City of Baltimore is the birthplace of Babe Ruth. They actually have a museum located in the original home where he was born.

It is also the place where I had one of my biggest sales.

"Jim, would you mind meeting with me privately in my Chambers?"

Mayor Kurt L. Schmoke had just invited me to leave the public hearing of the Board of Estimates where I had been testifying to the City Council Members in front of a small group of potential vendors, interested constituents and news reporters.

"Absolutely," I replied.

"And leave your boss behind."

My boss sat back down. My boss and I were bewildered at the request, but he nodded for me to go ahead with the Mayor.

I followed Mayor Schmoke into his Chambers which were just off to the right of the hearing room. He was a young Mayor for such a large city. At the time I was guessing I was about five years younger.

We sat down in two chairs in front of his desk and faced each other.

He began to speak. "Here we are at a crossroads. Your industry's largest competitor has been our vendor for the past ten years and made it through renewal bidding every two years. Now we are down to the end of the bidding process again and your small firm has us in a corner."

"What is the problem?" I asked.

"We know you can do the job better. But not cheaper." He replied.

I didn't respond immediately.

I could tell he had more to say and I didn't want to jump to the obvious conclusion.

This account would generate an estimated eighty-five million dollars in sales the first year of what would be a four-year contract. In coordination with the City accounting office our financial people had projected that the contract would grow by twelve to fifteen percent per year. This one account would increase our annual revenues by over twenty percent.

It would be a half-a-billion dollar account over the term of the contract.

It was a big sale … a very big sale.

I waited.

He spoke. "Next year is election year and I am running for a second term. I have two problems here. First, I must show my constituents that I have their best financial interests at heart. But, second, my constituents also include over three hundred independent pharmacies that under the terms of the incumbent's proposal will have to slash their margins in order to comply. So I have to decide between individual voters or small businesses."

I thought for a moment.

"Mr. Mayor?" I asked. "You must have a solution to propose to me or I wouldn't be here."

"I do." He said. "Small corner pharmacies are opinion centers of our neighborhoods. Pharmacists are held in higher esteem than doctors, and when not busy, they do not hesitate to express their opinions to their patients."

He stopped talking.

"So, if you treat the pharmacists fairly, they will carry the day for you come next November." My empathy for his dilemma was not lost on him.

"Exactly," He said. "And I am sure you saw the contingent of independent pharmacists at the hearing."

I had seen them and as a company we had been hearing from them. As a pharmacy benefit management company we provided prescription drug plans through employers to their employees as part of their health insurance programs. The groups we serviced typically were self-insured. Many used large insurance carriers as claims processors and branded their products accordingly. But by the end of the day our clients covered their own claims.

Our job was to link all of the nation's pharmacies electronically so that claimants could walk into any pharmacy, present their ID Cards and buy their prescriptions at pre-determined copayments.

Bottom line, we also operated our own mail-service pharmacy, negotiated with pharmaceutical companies for deep discounts, provided aggregate claims data to our clients and consulted with them regarding disease management, health-care outcomes, and a myriad of other services.

We also negotiated with retail pharmacies as to how much they would be reimbursed for dispensing medications, substitution of generics and pricing drugs according to volumes expected. All of these economic pressures that we crammed into a pricing pressure cooker were designed to reduce prescription drug costs. But independent pharmacies were the most adversely affected.

The Mayor looked over his peaked fingers. "I want to go back in there and tell the Board of Estimates that I have negotiated an arrangement that will protect the margins of the independent pharmacists. And that you and your company have agreed to monitor the positive impact it will have on every neighborhood these pharmacies serve."

"So you asked my boss to stay out of the room because…?" I was a little confused.

"With all due respect to your CEO," He said apologetically, "it is because you are the one that will be quoted in the Baltimore Sun newspaper as our new Account Executive for Pharmacy Benefit Services. You are the one who will be providing me with the monthly report in person. And you are the one who won this business because you personally know every aspect of the contract we are going to sign because you designed it with me and my staff."

He paused.

"Congratulations, this is going to be a career builder for both of us." I smiled and shook his hand.

And it was.

The next day I was quoted in the Baltimore Sun as being a proponent of the independent pharmacies of Baltimore at the request of the Mayor. (Go ahead…look it up.)

The sales process to the Mayor's Chambers was an extraordinary one.

At the time I had been working closely with the mid-Atlantic Regional Manager of our company because he had several very large (elephant-hunter size) prospects he was working on. John was a good guy, one of our older sales people, but relatively new to our business. His wisdom and demeanor was appreciated by his clients. But he followed the techniques I listed in Chapter One with every client. They are worth repeating here and I do so in dedication to John:

1. Unsolicited business must be humanized as soon as possible. Get in front of the buyer(s).

2. Once in front of your buyer(s) try your best to listen to why they are buying. For good salesmen this is very difficult. For great salesmen it is imperative.

3. Introduce up-line management as soon as possible through a positive introduction. If you do not believe in or trust your boss, sell for somebody else. No matter what the product buyers must be given the opportunity to believe that it is you and the company that stand behind your promises.

4. Return their phone calls by the end of the day (their time).

5. If you do not know the answers to their questions, tell them immediately. No hesitation, no vacillation no equivocation.

I dedicate them to John because shortly after he brought me in to help him with the City of Baltimore bidding process he was diagnosed with eye cancer which soon moved to his brain.

He was gone within a few short months.

He died just after we had won the City's half-billion dollar contract.

More than any other profession, sales touches the most human of emotions. The interactions between all parties to a sales transaction are usually pushed to some emotional limit.

Even the easiest of sales, the so called "slam dunks" carry expectation and doubt on both sides.

In this case John had developed a close enough rapport with the client that explaining his retirement from the account due to his medical reason was not only appropriate but of grave concern to the people we were working with at the City.

When he was forced to step out of the account we had only just attended the pre-bid conference. He had attended with an eye patch. At that time he was still awaiting his diagnosis, but was having problems with balance. But he had already "humanized" us as a company of individuals, met with members of the buying committee and introduced me (kind of his boss) to the process.

But while we kept a vigil for John, I was in the process of learning new sales techniques as I worked on this account.

Like many government accounts, the City of Baltimore required that a minimum of twenty-two percent of the contract had to be awarded to minority businesses: twenty percent to "African American minority business" and two percent to "women's minority" business.

I first heard of the situation at the pre-bid conference when the bid requirements were handed out to all thirty of the potential bidders. They also gave us a list of "approved" contractors. Then, and much to my surprise, as we walked out of the conference we were confronted with dozens of minority business owners who pushed business cards and brochures our way. It was a first for me, but still left me perplexed.

Winning this account was going to be a real long-shot. But bringing in two other partners as part of the sales cycle was going to make it even more difficult.

I have always considered sales situations like surgery. While there are nurses, anesthesiologists, interns, residents and other technicians in on the surgery, there can only be one lead surgeon. Someone has to call the shots, direct the procedures and take full responsibility for the end result.

Attorneys follow much the same strategy when in the courtroom. Sitting second chair really means second chair.

If a sales executive invites me to join them on sales calls we always determine who will take the lead (usually them because it is their account) and who would follow. It is a strategy of courtesy that does not go un-recognized by the buyer. Further, the "second chair" recognizes that the "surgery" is not theirs. And anything they want to do, add, or respond to is only as a compliment to the surgeon.

But now I had to find partners in a deal from a list of hundreds that I did not know.

So I tried a proven sales technique.

I asked my client to help me.

What a stroke of genius.

She already had a short list prepared and even helped me schedule interview appointments. In essence we did a pre-bid conference for subcontractors. I knew what areas of our contract we could best subcontract. But the most valuable part of the exercise was watching the ultimate buyer. Her body language and interest gave me the lead. It was like "American Idol" for subcontractors and she was Paula Abdul.

The most critical factor was the relationship it helped me build with the client. We actually were choosing my partners before I had been chosen as the vendor.

And because both the African American minority contractor and the women's-minority vendor were local businesses they were always available to attend meetings to add to the momentum of the sale.

Even more important, I invited the subs to help construct the proposed contract. The truth of the matter was that they did not know our business, so I asked the buyer to join in the meeting also. The Women's Minority business printed our educational materials for the program and the African American minority business processed hardcopy claims. But we asked the client to help us construct the language according to how best the contract would be awarded.

What began as a dilemma ended as a coup.

And the coupe de grace was winning the account.

With the help of many others I hit one out of the park just like Babe Ruth.

So here are five more proven sales techniques:

1. When you are brought in as the "boss" allow your sales executive to take the lead. Respect the surgeon.

2. When confronted with new obstacles ask the client to help you solve the problem.

3. Involve the potential buyer in writing the contract.

4. In a highly political environment recognize that the "spin" is up to the client.

5. Do not dwell on personal issues or exploit tragedies with your prospects. But do not discount them either.

Chapter 3

Paying for "Influence" is Worth it!

The question should be,
is it worth trying to do,
not can it be done.
- Allard Lowenstein, American diplomat

Two of my most interesting sales careers started from contacts I made at church. Sales and jobs in "sales" are made through networking... everywhere.

Like you, I am tired of the word "networking". But for lack of a better one I can tell you that extraordinary sales people talk to everyone they meet wherever they are about something.

Introverts like to call us "networkers", "extroverts" and a few of them even find us annoying.

Fortunately introverts rarely express their annoyance because they are too introverted so we rarely know the few we annoy.

But this circular observance aside, while attending church one Sunday I saw someone I had not met before and introduced myself. Turns out he had just accepted a job in the Philadelphia area as a Vice President of Sales for a mail-service pharmacy and he was looking for Regional Sales Executives.

A week later I had joined five other newly hired Regional Sales Executives in a company and industry none of us understood. And neither did our Vice President of Sales, the one I met at church. But he had been a client of this company and that is why they hired him.

We were all hired to replace a team of independent contractors that had been representing the company for the previous five years.

The VP of Sales posted a map of the United States on the wall and divided it into five regions and then asked, "Who wants which territory?"

One of us asked if we had to relocate, and he assured us that we would not. But obviously extensive travel would be required.

The only woman on our team asked if she could take the East Coast. She had lived and worked that corporate market for years and it made sense. We all nodded our approval.

I then asked who our primary target market was.

The VP answered that we would be going after Fortune 500 companies, insurance companies, unions, states and municipalities.

We talked about each of these vertical markets and after some discussion I asked if I could have the mid-West: Pittsburgh to Minneapolis including Cleveland, Chicago and South through St. Louis.

It was winter and everyone looked at me like I had three heads.

After getting a consensus I then told them why. This territory, which had been called the "rust-belt" contained more Fortune 500 companies and insurance companies than any other territory on the board. I was disappointed that the territory did not include any states with palm trees. But I figured if things went well I would be able to afford to visit palm trees whenever I wanted. So, yet another technique of salesmanship: know your stuff before you make a commitment.

I knew about this territory only because of a semi-interesting report I had seen on PBS about industry in America. Amazing what an aspiring sales person remembers.

For the first month on the job I researched lists of companies in the territory. This was well before the internet so I was booking hours at the local public library, reading the Wall Street Journal, Business Week and Newsweek. While doing this I recognized a couple of the accounts that we had on the books and asked my boss how we got them. He told me they came in through one of the independent contractors that had been selling for us in that territory. So I asked him if I could contact him. He told me to go ahead, but that he had agreed to limit his future sales to West of the Mississippi.

His name is Lance and I gave him a call. He knew of course what the company was doing, wasn't real excited about being pushed out of the east, but was willing to meet with me the next week when he was scheduled to be in Detroit.

It was the mid-eighties and Detroit was booming. American Motors had not yet been bought out by Chrysler and the auto companies were some of the largest employers in the country. Lance had sold a mail-order prescription program to American Motors and was in town to meet with the Auto Workers Union to see if they would help him gain entry to Chrysler. At the time I was in my mid-thirties and Lance was about five years younger. He knew the product, had several satisfied clients and several prospects that he was going to have to walk away from. We hit it off right away and I told him that I would try to convince management to leave him in on the deals he was working if he would partner with me on closing them. I had been in sales long enough to know that taking a little bit of something was way better than a whole lot of nothing.

So my first sale with my new job was to sell the boss on re-visiting his decision to cut-out Lance. I would place my commission package on the line and guarantee that the company would gain the sales control they wanted.

He bought it and we went to work.

Lance won the Chrysler business which I did not share with him. But he introduced me to his union contacts and we expanded the American Motors account and won Volkswagen of America. But more important, it helped me develop a strategic model for large accounts.

I call it "Influence Marketing".

This strategy played out several months later when I received a call from a couple of guys from Cleveland.

Sam and Dave were life insurance agents that specialized in selling key-man life insurance to executives of Fortune 500 companies. They had read an article about mail-order pharmacy plans and found a small ad we ran in a trade journal. Their call was routed to me because they were in my territory.

Their first question was "is mailing prescription drugs legal?"

At the time this was a growth industry. There were only three competitors and very few prospects even knew of the business proposition.

I met with Sam and Dave and within an hour we had discovered that with my ability to bring product they could "network" me into broker and consultant friends of theirs in Columbus, Toledo, Chicago, St. Louis, Minneapolis and Puerto Rico. Each of these strategic partners had clients who were CEOs, CFOs, and Board Members of the biggest companies in America.

"What about product training?" I asked.

"Screw product training." Dave said. "We are like pigs on ice here. If we can't do it standing up we will do it sitting down."

Sam piped in, "Look, your product is simple. Our guys will walk you in to the decision maker and you make the sale. If you need us to be the hammer, just make the call."

I picked up the phone and called my boss. Told him I would give up eighty percent of my commission if we could bring these guys and their partners on board. My success with Lance had proven that I could control the sales process. And their impressive list of prospects blew him away.

So now, in addition to Lance's prospects I had Sam and Dave's prospects, plus their strategic partners in seven other major cities.

I started to live on airplanes.

Deploying the strategy involved coordination, dedication and preparation. The industry was still in its infancy and each sales presentation was an educational presentation. First I had to tell the clients how mail-service prescription drugs were indeed legal and then convince them that it would bring savings to them and their employees.

I would spend a week at a time in Chicago with Tom, a week with Tim split between Toledo and Columbus, Sam and Dave had contacts in Dayton and Minneapolis and Dave's cousin was the Attorney General of Puerto Rico and best friends with the CEO of Triple S (Blue Shield of Puerto Rico). Palm trees already!

In the meantime I found other similar strategic partners that could walk me in to major decision makers and word was on the street that I could bring product to benefits brokers that would give them new credibility with existing clients and open the doors to new clients for them.

During the next two years through deployment of this strategic "Influence Marketing" plan we closed deals with the likes of Borden Foods, Kraft, Blue Cross of Ohio, Central Benefits Blue Cross, Eaton, Lubrizol, Blue Shield of Puerto Rico, City of Columbus, Union Central Life, and about two dozen others. It was a heady time. And all this even though the average sales cycle was six months from introduction to implementation. This was before laptops and power point presentations. I carried 35 mm slide trays and a heavy projector, (in addition to my golf clubs and swim trunks). Made great friends, had a great time and my clients knew that I loved what I was doing. These were sales-career-changing years for me and pivotal years for my strategic partners.

The little company I had been introduced to after a chance meeting at church grew so fast that it was bought off by a bigger company. I was offered the position of VP of Sales by the new owners but received a better offer from a competitor. Everyone should have an experience like this. The company that wanted to hire me away actually showed up with their CEO and legal counsel to negotiate a deal with my current employer. I felt like a major league baseball player. There were non-disclosures and non-competes to sign, a signing bonus and a whole new set of opportunities.

Sam and Dave started their own company and offered me a position with them. I didn't want to move to Cleveland but they remain good friends.

Lance took his commissions and started another company that we later worked joint accounts through. He too remains one of my best friends.

In future chapters I will revisit some of these techniques, but here are the next five:

1. Never underestimate your own ambition

2. Product knowledge is important but not as important as you may think.

3. Strategic "Influence Marketing" is always worth dividing up the profits!

4. Enjoy the sales process and your clients will enjoy buying from you

5. Make friends along the way. They always pay off.

Look within, for within is the wellspring of virtue, which will not cease flowing, if you cease not from digging.
- Marcus Aurelius

Chapter 4

Admire the Attire!

**Being defeated is often only a temporary condition.
Giving up is what makes it permanent.**
- Marilyn vos Savant, columnist and very smart person

"So Jim, how many sales can you and your team close in the first twelve months?"

He was Chairman of the Board and had founded the company ten years earlier.

"None" I replied.

"Good answer." He responded with a smile. "Now go out and surprise me."

He started to walk away, but turned back to me and said, "Nice suit."

The life of a corporate sales executive is a culmination of a whole lot of elements and we will cover over a hundred of them in this book. But I got a little ahead of myself in some of the previous chapters. Let me say right here that looks and grooming matter. This doesn't mean that every sales executive has to be plagued with obsessive compulsive disorder, but a marginal degree of narcissism and vanity in a controlled manner never hurts.

Four decades of meeting the public in every conceivable business setting has given me a degree of understanding. There have been a number of changes in both attire and demeanor.

When I was first hired into the corporate world as Assistant Vice President of a large corporate insurance brokerage firm the "Secretaries" and "Administrative Assistants" all addressed me as "Mr. Thompson" even though I was only twenty six years old and most of them were older than me. Of course I addressed them as "Ms. Whatever". We also never took our suit jackets off outside of our private offices, and always left them on when anyone came into our offices. I was reminded of this recently when President Obama set new standards and raised some eyebrows by removing his jacket while holding Cabinet meetings in the Oval Office.

Styles have changed: wide lapels, narrow lapels, wide ties, thin ties, starched white shirts, colored shirts with monochromatic ties, designer suits, baggy suits, executive over-the calf socks. And for women we have seen it all: panty-hose, bare legs, pants suits, practical shoes, three inch heels, mini-skirts, calf length dresses, big hair, curls, huge ribbon bow ties. All have come, gone and come again.

And there have been regional differences. I have had clients from the North Slope of Alaska to Puerto Rico. From Hawaii to Maine, Mississippi to Minnesota. I even spent three years in Japan where Japanese businessmen still dress the same now as they did in the sixties.

I have attended business meetings where we spent hours trying to decide what to wear at sales conferences. One conference we even offered free shoe shines at our booth. Only to be disappointed that everyone showed up in their running shoes or boat shoes.

A company I worked for was the target of a sexual harassment suit after we talked to a young sales executive regarding her wardrobe of low-cut tops and short skirts. Unfortunately she was a sales executive I had inherited when we bought a new company and I was the one that had to talk to her. HR gave me a script to use and assigned a female witness in the room. Didn't matter. We still got sued.

Her lawyer claimed that since she was a native of Southern California she needed to dress this way in order to be competitive in her environment. At the time our home office was on Long Island and our workplace was extremely conservative.

We still got sued.

So, here is the rule of thumb. Something I learned back when I was in my twenties and have found always to be successful. Always dress like the President of the United States. It is never over the top. Even if you are in the record business, entertainment, or engineering you will be respected. And remember, even the President plays basketball. And

President's have golfed, rode horses, played touch football and sailed. All of their attire is appropriate for those places. Knowing what to wear and when to wear it is important.

I train horses, snow ski, sail, ride my motorcycle and go to church. I also worked as an extra in Hollywood. Because of my look I was usually cast as a doctor, lawyer, FBI agent or business executive. But I was also cast as a boxing trainer, a cowboy, a Black Jack Dealer and in many other character roles. But for my headshots they wanted me in a conservative suit.

Coincidentally CNN reported recently that in our recession-driven environment the days of casual Friday are waning and that the traditional conservative business suit is the last bastion of "keeping your job".

Over the past three decades I have been to virtually every home office of every major company in the country. Whether it was casual Friday or a weekend retreat I showed up dressed for business. Granted, many times I received an invitation to take off my jacket. But my shirt was always crisply starched and wrinkle-free.

For years I shopped at Brooks Brothers. But also have a collection of not so expensive suits that fit me well, are always clean and pressed and look good on me. I also have a fresh tux in my closet. Don't use it as much as I would like. But then again, I live at a ski resort most of the year, and well, you get the point.

Ladies, my co-writer and editor came from corporate America and has been teaching MBA courses for over a decade.

Her advice?

Know the culture you work in. Unless you are working on Fifth Avenue forget what you see in Cosmo, Vanity Fair or the other magazines. Look at TV anchors and the women on the Weather Channel.

Also, target your market. Surprisingly, most of the corporate sales I made were either to women or women were involved in the process. My customers were Senior Benefits Managers, Human Resources Managers and Benefits Committees, politicians and yes, also women in labor. For me dressing conservatively and clean kept the focus on the meeting not on the accessories.

Both men and women look at watches. Expensive, but subtle is the rule.

My first job out of college was to manage a men's clothing store. It wasn't a Brook's Brother's. But I learned how a suit is designed to fit. If you don't know how to get a properly fitted suit, it is worth at least one trip to a custom men's store even if you don't lay out that amount of cash. Have them fit you for a suit and listen to what they have to say. Then when you go buy one off-the-rack you will know how to fit it. Disregard the size on the label. Just make sure that it fits you correctly: sleeves showing a little cuff, pant cuff between your heel and top of shoe, front coat button closed without pulling the back vent open and tie clean and spot-free.

Some people still call me old-school. I still have a white handkerchief in my breast pocket when I wear a white shirt. Not in a Denny Crane sort of way for you Boston Legal Fans, but more subdued. And just a heads up: if you are selling to women, make sure the hands are clean, nails trim and clean, a good haircut and facial hair neat, trim and fresh.

People admire the attire! Yes, dress for who you sell to. But by keeping it conservative they become the focus.

These techniques still never fail me and have worked from President Kennedy to President Obama:

Dark suits, white or light shirts, conservative ties. Dress like the President of the United States, or if a woman, like TV anchorwomen. CNN, Fox or CNBC are excellent choices. If that is too lofty for you, and you only sell in your state, Google your Senators and dress like they do.

1. Understated exudes confidence

2. Clean is mandatory. Hands, hair, face and shoes. Polished shoes are never old-fashion. I always carry one of those quick-polish pads in my brief-case. And don't hesitate to hit your brief-case with it either.

3. Dress for the culture and for the event. I own five pair of Cowboy boots, but other than when I am training my horses or hanging around the rodeo I leave them in the closet. I have dozens of clients in Texas, New Mexico, Atlanta and other places who wear them with their business suits. But I always

remember: they are the customer and can wear whatever they want. It helps that I know the difference between Tony Llama and Justin, Anaconda and eel. But knowing what to recognize and what to leave unnoticed can be covered in an entire book

You were born an original.
Don't die a copy.
- John Mason, author

CHAPTER 5

What I Learned
From Selling Ice Cream Cones!

All the joy the world contains
Has come through wishing happiness for others.
All the misery the world contains
Has come through wanting pleasure for oneself.
- Indian philosopher-poet Shantideva

On a whim I purchased a Baskin-Robbins franchise. At the time I was a young Assistant Vice President of a property casualty insurance brokerage firm that specialized in very large accounts.

Buying the Baskin-Robbins franchise wasn't exactly a whim. In fact the application process for purchasing the franchise was not unlike trying to qualify to adopt a child. And the vetting process was far more intense than those of Presidential appointments. Were I not so young and ambitious I might have stepped aside. But I hung in there with my spouse and a partner and his spouse. I had worked in retail before, but owning and operating a national fast-food franchise was to be a whole new experience. Making sales a single-scoop cone at a time was a far cry from where my "real" career was headed. But if you have never owned your own business you have never really had blood pump through your veins.

Our first day open for business was the day after Thanksgiving. Retailers call it "Black-Friday": the day retail sales finally break-even for the year. Our store was in a mall and we had no idea what to expect.

We ran out of ice-cream!

Christmas shoppers wearing their winter coats against the late fall Pennsylvania winds would come into the mall. After an hour or so of shopping while still wearing or carrying their coats, would have them looking for something cold and comforting. And there we were: all thirty-one flavors plus sundaes, shakes, banana splits, floats and other delicacies. We were an oasis of satisfaction in an orgy of pre-Christmas anxiety. And from that day forward through the five years that I co-owned and operated this franchise my sales and marketing expertise grew exponentially.

What can you learn about selling ice cream cones that you can use in making sales of any size?

Almost everything!

From the very first customer I realized that people love to buy when they get to make a choice.

This sounds pretty fundamental; but undisputable.

Again, we had thirty-flavors to choose from and with seasonal flavors we sometimes had up to forty. We even offered free tastes of whatever product they wanted to buy before we sold them. Some people would want to try several. Others never would even try something new no matter how glowingly we described the smooth creamy flavor or the added ribbons of flavor or the crispy chunks of candy.

Amazingly our most popular flavor was vanilla! And not only was it the most popular, but we sold ten times more vanilla than any other flavor. Go figure! Can it be true that most people, given the choice, would choose the same thing as most other people?

It was. And it still is.

So after vanilla then what?

The next five most popular flavors were strawberry, chocolate, chocolate chip, mint chip and butter pecan. Combined with vanilla these produced over fifty percent of our gross sales.

And so it was in making sales for me.

When I won the fifty million dollar contract for the State of Montana Employment System I was also awarded contracts with the other eight largest employers in Montana. The price and terms were the same as the State but each of them had the choice of how their plans could be designed at no additional cost. The product I was selling was a prescription drug plan that would be used by employees and retirees. It would be integrated into their health insurance programs and they could have a choice of hundreds of different plans. They could have copayments different for brand name drugs, generic drugs, mail-service drugs and or specialty medications. They had the choice of what drugs would be included or excluded. They could also choose how they wanted the actual cards designed for their members to use. They could decide which pharmacies would participate in the plan. In essence I gave them each individually the opportunity to design their programs from a huge menu of options.

But, with very few exceptions, they asked, "What is the State doing, and can we just do it that way?"

Of course, some ten years before I sold the State of Montana their program I had learned from selling ice cream cones that people love to have choices...and then almost always choose the same thing.

Early in my sales career, even before I sold men's clothing I learned that giving a potential buyer two choices was always better than the choice of buying or not buying. So the whole Baskin-Robbins scenario was not surprising.

This is called the "either-or" close.

"Would you like to buy the red car or the blue car?"

Not:

"Would you like to buy a car?"

But I had also been taught that giving a prospect more than three choices was a deal breaker, too confusing and doomed to a non-sale. According to my experience, both over the ice cream counter and in the board room, this was almost never true. In fact, customers usually want to know that you have the agility and acumen to provide a broad spectrum of choices even though they usually hone in on one or two.

And of course the "up-sale" can never be overlooked.

"How about two scoops today? Have you ever tried a scoop of peanut-butter and chocolate with this scoop of pralines and cream?" I would ask.

"Oh no...I never mix chocolate with vanilla." She responded.

"Oh, then the butter-pecan would be a better mix for you with the pralines and cream."

"Hmmm." She replied. "That does sound good."

And so the simple "up-sell" choice happens every day in every fast-food restaurant.

"Would you like fries with that?" Has not only become common-place, but fodder for the funkiness of contemporary language.

One of my sales executives had won the business of a very large insurance company. They insured well over two million members nationwide and we were going to roll out a new prescription drug program through their several market segments over an eighteen month period. I had joined the sales executive through the finalist presentations and after being awarded the business we were out to dinner with the Group Sales Manager, the CFO and the VP of Strategic development. It was a very cold night in Omaha, but we were enjoying a nice steak. I turned to the CFO, thanked him for joining us and then asked him, "How many employees do you have?"

"About fifteen thousand in the U.S." He replied. "And we have about two thousand ex-patriots in English-speaking countries throughout the world."

"Do you provide prescription benefits for all these employees?" I asked

"Sure." He said. "We have one of the most generous plans in our industry."

I thought for a moment and then said, in a very casual manner, "As Jane has so excellently illustrated, it looks like we are going to cut your prescription drug claim costs for your insurance clients by about fifteen percent. But it looks like we have overlooked your own employees."

He seemed to stop in mid-bite.

"We can do that?" he said.

"Sure can." I replied. "How about your retirees? That is where your highest costs are. After all, Medicare covers their other medical costs. You are covering their prescriptions, doctor visits and durable medical equipment, right?"

By now he had stopped eating all together.

Up until that point, all of the executives we had been selling our product to were only concerning with their insurance products for their group and individual business lines. No one in the room had a vested interest in the employees of the company.

This ended up being a twenty million dollar up-sell!

It wasn't quite as easy as asking for him to try another scoop of ice cream. But the psychological positioning was the same. Why wouldn't he want more of what he had already bought?

We didn't seal the deal over that steak dinner. In fact it took us another year to get the sale made. Turns out the HR Manager had a close relationship with the incumbent vendor and eventually the program had to go out to bid for us to get back to the table. But we did, and the CFO did not forget that it was our brief conversation that had spawned the opportunity for him to improve his bottom line.

One final example of the microcosm of marketing fast food that I carried into making larger sales was "demographic preferences".

Tastes change, preferences change, mores change, but at any given point in time all of these things do matter.

Over three decades ago when I was scooping ice cream on weekends and meeting with corporate clients during the week the phrase "demographic preferences" walked up to me every day. Teenage girls almost always ordered mint-chip (unless we had Pink Bubblegum), people over the age of fifty almost always ordered butter-pecan, soccer moms almost always ordered Pralines and Cream (unless they were pregnant and then they bought Jamoca-Almond-Fudge), African-Americans almost always ordered strawberry or vanilla and kids under five almost always ordered vanilla.

This was not profiling, it was "market intelligence".

Like any good business we kept track of this stuff. And like all good businessmen I was curious. Not as to "why" but, if true, how could I take advantage of this information. At the time I had a very good friend who worked as Regional Sales Manager for Duncan-Hines, the cake mix division. I told him of my observations. Just to see if he had similar information.

"Not sure about all of those demographics, but I can tell you that our chocolate cake mix sales south of the Mason-Dixon are only half of what they are up North."

This was an ongoing epiphany for me. As I developed "Influence Marketing" strategies throughout the country I recognized that using local influence peddlers was far more successful than hiring people and transferring them into a territory. The subtleties of culture, mores and geographic idiosyncrasies are not to be under-estimated, even at the highest corporate levels. And many of them are so innate to the native that they do not even know what they are a part of.

This is kind of like understanding that people in Mississippi do not know that Forrest Gump has an accent. But they recognize right away that the rest of us do.

About a year before the attack of nine-eleven on the World Trade Center I had been hired as Senior Vice President of Sales and Marketing for a company located on Long Island.

We were doing about four hundred million in sales, had just gone public and had decided to deploy two strategies: first to increase organic growth (make more sales) and second to make strategic acquisitions. I was involved in both strategies.

When I had arrived the company was just finishing the acquisition of a company out of Little Rock, Arkansas and during the next year we bought a company based in Tulsa, Oklahoma and started negotiations with a company in Albany, New York. Part of our acquisition strategy was to integrate corporate cultures. This is corporate-speak for finding out if we can work with each other.

As may be expected, the employees of the home office in Long Island thought the people in Little Rock were hicks. The people in Little Rock thought the people in Long Island were rude, the people in Tulsa were born again Christians (small company…only twenty employees) and were determined to convert the rest of us. Then I learned that people in Albany despise people within the shadows of New York City. Of course in our Long Island office we had employees commuting from New Jersey, Brooklyn, Yonkers, Manhattan, Connecticut and most other places within a fifty mile radius. We also had Catholics, Jews, Episcopalians, Seeks, Presbyterians, Blacks, Italians, Irish, Pakistani, and all of the wonderful variety of peoples that make up our country.

Oh, and buy the way, I had been raised in Utah and didn't even know how strange I was until I had moved to Philadelphia after college.

Conversations were pleasant on the surface, but a cynical revolution was festering at the water coolers.

Then came nine-eleven: it was a corporate tipping point for our combined companies. Those syrupy, slow speaking people from Little Rock, the extroverts from Tulsa and the up-Stater's from Albany were all on the phone with their counter-parts in Long Island expressing their concern and empathy. Our employees in Long Island were flabbergasted. They couldn't believe the outpouring of sympathy and genuine humanity of their corporate peers. Our New York staff members had spouses and other family members that were lost in the attacks. We also had "extended family" that worked for the Port Authority, Fire and Police Departments that were affected. And in all of this grief and anxiety our company took on a sense of unity.

It was a miracle.

I still have the memo that our CEO wrote to the company. My office was right next to his and he came to me before writing it.

I had been in Houston meeting with a prospect on nine-eleven. He waited for a week until I returned until he put out a formal statement to the company.

"I don't know what to do, or what I could say." He was sincerely concerned.

I had driven a rental car back from Houston, dropping off members of my presentation team in their respective offices in Tulsa then Little Rock.

"What are people saying to each other?" I asked.

"Well, the first day it was silence." He said. "Then the phones started to ring and the conversations have not stopped."

"I think this is a good thing."

"It is." He said. "And I don't want to mess it up."

"Then I would thank them all for being so supportive of each other." And he did.

Sales techniques from this chapter cross virtually all selling environments.

1. Let your customers know that you have a broad choice of products or solutions, but try to limit the best choices for their situation.

2. Most customers choose the same thing, but let them come to that conclusion on their own.

3. Up-selling only works if you try it.

4. Know the demographics of your marketplace and play to them with indigenous strategies

5. Be ready for cultural anomalies. By the end of the day we all have the same motivations, needs and emotions.

6. Sometimes good things happen under the worst of circumstances.

The only normal people are the ones you don't know very well.
- Joe Ancis, comedian

Chapter 6

What's That Noise?

"What's that noise?" My wife was standing in the doorway of the family room with her hands on her hips.

"It's NASCAR, and I've got it on surround sound." I had to yell in order for her to hear me.

"What's NASCAR?"

"It's kind of like hockey, except with cars. I think fans hope for a huge wreck." I had never watched it before, but had a vested interest in learning more about it.

"BLAM!'

Tires screeched, the sound of tearing metal ripped through the room and the sound of ambulances wailed."

It was a huge wreck. Within ten minutes it was confirmed; Dale Earnhardt, the undisputed king of NASCAR was dead.

I turned off the TV.

"Why did you turn it off? Didn't they have a big wreck? Isn't that why you were watching?"

"Well, sort of." I mumbled.

I didn't know Dale Earnhardt, but I felt sorry for him and his family.

I was also thinking about the fifty-thousand dollar check I had just cut from our marketing budget to kick off a quarter-million-dollar advertising campaign using NASCAR pit-crews as a metaphor for "Extraordinary Service at the Speed You Need."

I was worried that this was going to be a mistake.

Selling requires a myriad of elements. Most of which are more human than most people think. But corporate branding and imagery are contributing factors.

My challenge in creating expanded organic growth for the company was presented with three significant components:

- First, our company was small, unknown and morphing through the acquisition of three other companies

- Second, we had to prove that we were just as competent as our competitors, and

- Third, we had to define ourselves as a unique choice in a commoditized marketplace.

By then I had been in the pharmacy benefit management industry for over twenty years. The industry had gone through a classic growth algorithm from emerging products and services with less than five percent market penetration to standardized products and services, equivalent price points and a ninety-five percent market penetration. Clients had swapped vendors several times and the name of the game was to grow your company so that you could be bought out by the next bigger company, cash out and run away.

Basically the only thing left to be fought for was customer service. In the healthcare marketplace the most utilized component was and still is the prescription drug plan.

Everyone takes prescription medication. If the drug plan fails, even on the smallest scale, the plan sponsor (our customers) get calls from their employees, retirees, union members, constituents, etc. and the bidding process starts all over.

Companies do not like to change vendors.

The last thing they want is a revolt from their employees because their local pharmacy doesn't honor their drug card or their mail order prescription was lost in the mail.

Price is important.

But I had learned something about price and branding when I owned my fast-food franchise. During that time I had corporate clients all over the country. So while traveling I would always make a point to find the local Baskin-Robbins and check them out.

First I checked for cleanliness, order and courtesy. Then I checked for price. If cleanliness, order and courtesy were excellent, price did not seem to matter. So since my store was clean, orderly and my employees were courteous I knew I could charge whatever I wanted.

There were two other ice cream stores in our mall and I always priced my scoops higher. If I found a store anywhere in the country that had a price higher than mine I would return and raise my price. My partner, who was an accountant, took a hard gulp every time I did this. But he slowly learned that service counts and branding is king. People eat Baskin-Robbins ice cream because they love it. And because they love it, they are willing to pay for it.

Over the decades this has not been lost on the other fast food success stories: Krispy-Cream, Haagen-Dazs, Starbucks, Dunk'n Donuts (which is now jointly owned with Baskin-Robbins) and the list goes on.

I decided to take "Influence Marketing" from the sales force to the marketing department. Why not co-brand with a known entity?

As I looked at our competitors they all looked the same. Walking through trade shows I observed that their booths were different in name only. The bigger companies had bigger booths, but they had the same suite of offerings. Since we were in healthcare the colors of healthcare were prevalent: muted greens, blues and grays. There were people in white coats and walls be-speckled with pills, capsules, mortar and pestles. Words were the same.

I remembered in a sales meeting some years before with a different company we were asked to call all of our clients and ask them what set us apart from other companies. The responses were overwhelming and surprising. They liked the pens we gave them! Indeed, they were cool pens. They looked liked drug capsules and had a weight in one end. This caused them to stand up-right on a flat surface, but bobble like bobble dolls when flicked with a finger. Go figure. We were doing two billion dollars a year selling prescription drug plans and our clients liked our bobble pens!

I thought about bobble pens for this new company, but decided it was more of the same.

The pit-crew idea hit me when surfing the sports channels one night when I heard an announcer proclaim "these pit crews are something else! They have to get it right in less than ten seconds…and they only get one chance."

When I called in our ad agency I told them that I wanted them to come back with a slogan to fit. Then I went to my fellow senior staff members and asked them if they would buy into a pit-crew metaphor for each of their departments. Could we turn "best-practices" into "measureable results" using a pit-crew visual? Could we distinguish ourselves internally and externally as a company that could provide "Extraordinary Service at the Speed our customers need"? Before getting their answer I set up the conference room video system and showed them clips of the Tom Cruise classic racing movie "Days of Thunder". I played it loud and hollered over the pit-crew scenes. The Executive Staff were almost as excited as when I rolled out the campaign to our national sales force.

It blew them away.

By the next trade show we had put it all together. We showed up with NASCAR jackets, flags, a slot car game, and a surround-sound audio feed blaring the most recent NASCAR race.

"What's that noise?"

People came in crowds. Our booth was at least ten people deep throughout the conference. The big surprise was that with the death of Dale Earnhardt NASCAR had taken on even more popularity. The bigger surprise was that those most impressed with our campaign were women! These were the Benefits Managers, HR Professionals and others to whom we had targeted, but we had no idea how big of fans they were. In fairness, we did not have the budget to get co-branding rights from NASCAR so we had focused on the pit-crew concept. But the association was not lost on our prospects.

And the competition was watching too.

At the next trade show we had stepped up our campaign with actual racing video games and during the conference our largest competitor actually rented one just like ours from a local arcade and rolled it into their medicinal booth. Another competitor brought in a NASCAR driver to give autographs. But we had already made a mark.

Our advertising agency won a regional award for our campaign and we became known as "that company that has extraordinary service".

The campaign lasted for a year and then we went on to other things. But like any other deployment this campaign was not without its challenges. Being innovative in a mature market takes courage, but it also requires focus on fundamentals. Some of my sales executives started to lead with the brochure and forgot to show up with an inquisitive attitude. Not all prospects were as focused on service and speed. But they knew our table stakes. We were focused on service and we were different.

Within a year we passed the billion dollar mark in sales. Reaching this goal can be attributed to many components and over five hundred employees who were drawn together through campaigns, tragedies and extraordinary service.

Important sales techniques presented in this chapter include:

1. Innovation works but requires collaboration

2. Co-branding-by-association embracing contemporary trends can be defining

3. Stepping out of industry mores with proper branding supersedes pricing competition

4. Extraordinary Service is priceless, but you need to "sell it"

If the world seems cold to you, kindle fires to warm it.
- Lucy Larcom, poet

Chapter 7

Everything I Know
I Learned from a Home Office SOB

**A man is about as big
as the things that make him angry.**
- Winston Churchill

I have worked for and with a number of brilliant people in my life. And I don't just say this because they hired me.

This CEO was one of the best. He was a finance guy by training and frugal as they come. Twenty years after walking out of Wharton School of Business with his diploma he was still wearing the same pair of shoes his Dad had bought him as a graduation gift.

He was soft spoken, wise and precise.

On the other hand our CFO was brash, demanding, insulting, and if we were to throw in some medical acronyms he was also ADD, ADHD, and OCD. His administrative assistant put in twelve hour days and he expected the same of the rest of us.

If we had ten minutes left to get out a proposal that we had written and re-written twenty times, he would insist that we use the last ten minutes to re-write it again. And this was before e-mail, Blackberry's and cell phones! At that time we were faxing revisions on the funky old-school fax paper. In fact, when I had joined this company I went out and bought them their first PC. I had never used a PC before. But no one else had time to learn how to use one. Technology was catching up and I knew how to run my Apple. How much harder could a PC be?

I was hired the day before, handed a Request For Proposal (RFP) from Dow Chemical Company worth fifty million dollars and was told by the CFO that he wanted it finished and on his desk in three days. They had never sold a big account before and that is why I had been hired. Truth be known, I had never responded to an RFP before either. I had been out selling through my "Influence Marketing" network and never received an unsolicited request for proposal.

I was out of my element.

But I had taken the job with a highly incentivized compensation package and had my eyes wide open going in. This company was the smallest company I had worked for and I knew that it was going to be a lot of work.

What I didn't know was that regardless of the fact that by this time in my career I had gained a national reputation of closing big deals, my biggest challenge was going to be the man I worked for, not the clients I sold to. Fortunately, I went into the company like Gomer Pyle entering the Marines. I didn't know that latrine duty wasn't an honorable way to work my way into the good graces of my Sergeant! So I took his crap and went with it.

This CFO had originally recruited me to be the company's VP of Sales. I had declined the position because he wanted me to relocate to St. Louis. But, in declining the position I had proposed an alternative. I knew he wanted my skills, so I recanted them to him and sold him on the idea that he could have my skills unfettered by administrative issues. Plus, I would be willing to mentor whomever they brought in as VP of Sales.

He bought into the strategy.

Once on board, I found out that he had taken it as a personal failure not convincing me to move to St. Louis and accept the VP position. So in a maddeningly masochistic manner he loaded me down with performing about ten jobs descriptions at once, all compressed into the immediate task at hand.

The RFP that was sitting on my desk from DOW Chemical would be a fifty-million dollar contract. Our company currently had only twenty-five million in sales and twenty-million of that was from our parent company.

I looked at the two-hundred-page RFP on my desk. It had enough questions to spawn a five hundred page response.

I looked at the shiny new PC next to it.

I could hear the CFO in a ceiling-lifting argument with the woman who had been in line for the VP of Sales position before I showed up. He was berating her over the fact that she had let the DOW RFP sit on her desk for two weeks with no action. She was screaming at the top of her lungs that he had forced her to attend a trade conference last week. And that she was ready to resign over the fact that all of her work had been put on my desk.

I looked at my desk.

It was a long folding table that had been set up just inside the back outside door of the office. We only had fifty employees. But every time someone wanted to go out for a smoke, leave for lunch, go out for fresh air or come back from any of those errands the door behind me hit the back of my chair.

I plugged in the new PC.

It booted up, but the door behind me was glass and the glare from outside created a glare on my computer screen. I had to put on a baseball cap and sunglasses to see the screen.

By Thursday, after four fifteen-hour work days, I had finished the proposal. It was indeed over five-hundred pages plus twenty-five tabbed exhibits.

In less than a week I had learned more about every aspect of our company than any other employee. And, frankly, I learned more than the combined understanding of both the CFO and the CEO. Throughout the process I had interviewed all the department heads, called clients for references, analyzed utilization data, designed responses regarding "Best Practices" and "Corporate Governess". Since we were a mail-service pharmacy I also went through all the processing procedures with our Director of Clinical Pharmacy.

After ten years of successful selling I was finally learning what went on at the home office.

Up until that point I had refused to be intimidated by my ignorance.

But it was about to be pointed out to me.

Friday morning I put a copy of the finished product on the CFO's desk and also left one for the CEO. At that time they were sharing an office and the CEO was also running the parent company so he only came in two days a week.

The CFO started immediately bellowing from his office for re-writes and yelling out "who told you this stuff!"

The proposal had to be at DOW corporate headquarters by Monday afternoon. The plan was to get it to Federal Express by the Friday five pm cut-off time.

The yelling and demands for re-writes continued all day.

At four pm the CEO walked by and said, "Good work for the first one. The CFO has some changes he will get to you."

I guess he had learned to block out all the noise.

I was starting to sweat.

Sweating on the job was something I had been very accustomed to when I was a kid working on the farm. But sitting there in my Brooks Brothers suit and starched shirt sweating without moving a muscle was new to me.

At ten minutes to five the CFO slammed the proposal on my desk and told me that in spite of all the changes we had made throughout the day this was the biggest piece of crap he had ever read.

The deadline for FedEx was only two hours away.

Now I really started to sweat.

Whoever said "not to sweat the small stuff", never had so much small stuff to sweat all at the same time.

My coat was off, my sleeves were rolled up, my sunglasses and baseball cap were slipping off my head and the two administrative assistants were running back and forth between the CFO's office, my office and the copy machine. One of them was crying. I could tell it wasn't the first time.

It wasn't pretty.

Every change we made elicited another re-write.

Every re-write spawned a pagination change.

Every pagination change threw off our table of contents.

Every table of content change messed up our tabbed exhibits

At five minutes to seven we piled all eleven copies into my rental car and broke every traffic law between our office and the FedEx office.

We made it.

When I got back to the office with the surviving Administrative Assistant the CFO was still there. He was standing at my table.

"Here are more changes. Get these cleaned up and call DOW to let them know you are faxing them as an addendum."

We didn't get the DOW account.

They claimed we just weren't big enough to handle their business. But they wrote an extraordinary letter complimenting us on our proposal.

When the CFO received it he gave it to me and told me to throw it in the trash where it belonged.

From that point on, through the nine years I spent with the company he didn't change.

He wore out and ran off three Sales VPs. His Administrative Assistant quit and was rehired every week.

My proposal group grew to ten full time staff writers who I managed remotely from my home office when I wasn't on airplanes flying around the country selling.

The company grew from twenty-five million to its current revenues of over twenty billion.

After five years of reporting to this CFO while closing the company's largest accounts I finally sprung myself out to a Regional Territory Position.

Many of you may have a boss like this. Even in today's environment of "corporate appropriateness", "diversity training", "workplace environmental training", and "harassment litigation" there are still hard-driving SOBs that seem to slip through the HR strainer. But I learned some extraordinary techniques that made a huge difference in selling:

1. Take every opportunity to learn everything you can about your company and its products and services.

2. Writing well helps you sell well.

3. Your work can always be improved

4. Sweating at work is what they pay you for.

5. Working for an SOB can help you prevent being one yourself

**Tolerance implies no lack of commitment to one's own beliefs.
Rather it condemns the oppression or persecution of others.**
- John F. Kennedy

Chapter 8

The Ten Minute Presentation

**When one door closes another door opens;
but we often look so long and so
regretfully upon the closed door,
that we do not see the ones which open for us.**
- Alexander Graham Bell

My proposal staff had pulled out all the stops on this one. We had been given the opportunity to bid on business for the State of Maine. It was our first State bid. Winning a State bid could mean winning another State bid and also would set us up for local municipalities, counties and maybe a shot at some Federal business.

We had made it to the first cut. There were only five of us left out of the original twenty-five.

This part of the "finalist letter" was great.

The last sentence was disturbing: "Each finalist will have ten minutes to make a presentation to our selection committee. Your scheduled time is attached."

We were scheduled last at four-thirty pm a week from Friday.

My first thought was that this would be impossible. The RFP had been huge in both scope and detail. We knew from industry reports that the State of Maine was embroiled in significant litigation against their incumbent and a class action suit had been filed by covered employees of the State against the State and their vendor.

I went into the CEOs office, showed him the letter and asked him what he wanted to do.

"We are going."He said.

"We?" I asked.

"Yes," he replied. "Me, you, the CFO and I want to bring our VP of Technology and our Clinical Director."

"We only have ten minutes." I replied. "Who is going to lead."

"We will wait and see who they have in the room."

"Sounds like a plan." I replied.

The good news was that I didn't need to put together a formal presentation. It was 1994 and the pre-power-point days. Back then it was all about thirty-five millimeter slides. Our local photography shop owner had put two kids through college taking pictures, making graphs and producing logo-splattered slides for us.

Nice to know I wasn't going to have to lug a projector and slide tray with me.

Since our presentation was late in the afternoon we planned to make the trip in one day. Had a nine AM flight booked out of St. Louis to Boston where would rent a car for all five of us and then drive the hundred and seventy three miles to Augusta.

The plane left about twenty minutes late, which was lucky for us because our CFO arrived late. He had gone into the office at five AM, had his Administrative Assistant there by five-thirty and had put together a thirty-page pricing spread sheet if our ten minutes was miraculously extended to five hours.

This was no surprise to the rest of us and we had all arranged our seats so we didn't have to sit by him and get sucked into re-working the numbers for the umpteenth time.

We arrived an hour and a half late into Boston. It was one-thirty and we only had three hours to drive a hundred and seventy three miles. This included getting through Boston out of Massachusetts across Maine, taking the right exit for Augusta, finding the State Capital Annex and the right room for the meeting. This was before GPS and Map-quest. We were using a map from the car rental counter.

Since I lived in Philadelphia which was four hundred miles closer to Maine than St. Louis I was chosen to drive. It made no sense to me.

But at least I didn't have to sit in the back seat with the CFO and CEO who were commencing to tear apart the financial spreadsheets.

We arrived at the bidding-room door at four-twenty pm. Ten minutes early. Once again I had broken into a full weight-room sweat while just sitting and driving. The three executives in the back seat had given "back-seat driving" a whole new definition.

There were three other people sitting on chairs in the hall.

We knocked.

A person came to the door and apologized.

"Sorry, we are running about twenty minutes late. Looks like you won't be up until four-fifty. But we have to be out of hear by five o'clock so be ready." She stepped back into the room.

The other three people each represented the other three bidders before us.

One by one they were called in and one by one they left. I timed them. They each only got ten minutes.

At ten minutes to five we were called in.

There were eight committee members.

I did a quick calculation and figured that by the time they had introduced themselves and we had introduced ourselves the meeting would be over.

One of them introduced us to the rest by giving the name of our company and reiterating the fact that the meeting had to be adjourned by five pm. She then introduced each of the panel members.

No finance people.

There were two people from HR, two people from the State's Employee Benefits department, two union representatives, the State's Employee Benefits Consultant and the State Attorney General.

I gulped.

The CEO turned to me and nodded.

I gulped again.

Guess he had decided I was leading the discussion.

I wasted no time and introduced each of us, ending with the CEO.

'I then turned and asked the panel, "Why are we here?"

"Finally," The Chief Benefits Officer said. "Everyone else we have seen tried to cram a sales presentation into their ten minutes. Nice to know you folks want to know what we need."

There was a slight chuckle from his peers and the same from our people.

He had a definite down-state demeanor. Fortunately I had known some people from that part of Maine and also had a broker that vacationed on Bar Harbor. I knew enough to know that even though my bosses were from the "show-me" state, folks from Maine not only wanted to be shown, but also convinced.

I held our show-and-tell back until called on.

Surprisingly the Attorney General spoke.

"You are here because your contract appears to be the easiest one for me to litigate if you screw up."

Again there was a little chuckle from that side of the table.

I maintained eye contact with the Attorney General and watched the other panel members through my peripheral vision. I had no idea what my people were doing.

I knew at that point anything we said in defense would either appear to be self-serving or off point.

Without looking down, I took out my yellow pad and said, "Tell me exactly what you mean."

I heard my team rustling their notepads open and their pens started scratching as the Attorney General started to speak.

For the next eight minutes he spoke and we wrote. I only interrupted for a couple of clarifications.

The State of Maine had been in a law-suit with the incumbent vendor that had been dragging on for over a year.

Turns out that the litigation had all landed on the Attorney General's desk and he had become far more of an expert in the pharmacy benefit program than any of the line staff members. Their hired-gun "benefits consultant" even seemed clueless as to some of the highly technical issues that had spawned the law suits and the bidding process.

At five pm one of the HR Staff members interrupted the AG's litany of litigious issues to announce that the meeting had to be adjourned.

She thanked us for our time and we folded up our yellow pads and walked out of the room.

The first ten minutes of the ride back to Boston was silent. Frankly I knew that I had assumed the right strategy. I was also grateful that our CFO hadn't stood up and tore into the Attorney General for the broad-based accusations he had made against our industry as a whole. But still, in the back of my mind I wasn't sure if I would have a job by the time we got home.

Finally the CEO spoke.

"Jim," he said. "You did a hell of a job in there."

"Thanks." I replied.

And then all hell broke lose.

The CEO and CFO started to tear into their yellow pads. Repeating back and forth what the Attorney General had said. What they had wanted to respond with. Why they hadn't. What they thought they should have said. Questioning each other as to how he could have learned so much about the hidden costs and profits of our industry.

For the next three hours and even the four hours on the plane they went back and forth. It became mind-numbing blah-blah-blah to the rest of us. They kept trying to bring me in to confirm their assumptions. Usually I would just nod or reply, "You heard him."

Two weeks later we were notified that we had won the business.

Two weeks after that the award was rescinded. The incumbent had sued the State for unfair bidding practices and the litigation precluded the award.

We missed a bullet on this one. The litigation continued for two more years and the contract became the tar-baby of the industry.

There were several important sales techniques learned in winning and losing this contract:

1. Always show up with your guns loaded

2. Keep the safety on

3. Be prepared for someone else to be the buyer

4. When you ask, be prepared to listen

5. Selling is sometimes done by the buyer

6. Sometimes a loss is a win

Chapter 9

Never Take a Full Backswing
In a Tiled Bathroom

**The real joy of life is in its play.
Play is anything we do for the joy and love of doing it,
apart from any profit, compulsion, or sense of duty.
It is the real joy of living.**
- Walter Rauschbusch, Theologian

I Confess!

I love to play golf.

I train Arabian horses and ride them in Western parades and rodeos.

I ride my motorcycle through scenic Southern Utah.

I fish high mountain lakes for cut-throat and native trout and catch and release them.

I snow ski and am taking snow-boarding lessons.

I pull out all the stops (literally) and love to blow people out of the pews playing church organs.

I can sit on warm beaches and read for days on end.

I have an ATV and take "green" trails to look at petro glyphs and old Native American ruins.

I love to go to the movies and the louder the sound system the better.

I know every episode of Seinfeld. I leave the TV on in my office regardless of what I am working on.

For a year I took a sabbatical from watching TV. I didn't have time because during that year I was working as an extra in Hollywood and although a TiVo'd a bunch of stuff, watching how the sausage was made kind of took the luster off the breakfast. But, if you look closely you will see my bald head bobbing and weaving through episodes of "Shark", "ER", "Desperate Housewives", "Big Love", "Boston Legal", "Las Vegas", "CSI New York". "Curb Your Enthusiasm", "Stand-Off", Gilmore Girls", and dozens of others. I also wander through several movies including: "Rendition", "The Charlie Wilson Wars," and others that never made it to the big screen and went right to DVD.

I live with anticipation for visiting theme parks. Not a huge roller-coaster fan, but love to grab some kids and take them on all the rides.

I am a die-hard Philadelphia Eagles Fan.

I go to concerts ranging from Bocelli to Bette Midler.

Dogs are God's gift to all mankind and I share them whenever I can.

I am addicted to dominos and always have a Sudoku book in my pocket, my briefcase or by my bed.

Fast cars are and always will be a part of my life.

Marching bands make me cry with pride and patriotism.

God has always been the center of my life.

I spent thirty-two months living and working as a missionary in Japan and learned that until you live in another country you cannot appreciate the United States of America.

Almost every day I post photos to "Facebook", "MySpace", "Twitter", "LinkedIn" and other social networks.

I write down everything I do and then write about everything I do.

I have been sailing in the calm Caribbean and the hostile Pacific.

I like almost every food.

If I had a chance to wear a tux once a week I would do so.

I have done business in every state in the country.

I have gained and lost forty pounds. And it has not returned in three years.

I have fallen in love and had my heart broken.

I have been a millionaire.

I have been poor enough to live off of the good will of friends and family.

Cooking is something I like to do for people.

I have never missed a High School Class Reunion.

I am happiest when I am around other people.

I gain power and confidence the more I learn.

I have been on a hot air balloon ride and found it incredibly non-exhilarating.

I have lived on a catamaran for a week in the Caribbean and snorkeled off several islands.

I have been to almost every National Park from Glacier in Montana to Coral Reef off the North Coast of the Florida Keys.

I hate to argue but love to listen to opinions.

I have written and published books on diverse subjects.

I love to tell stories and listen to stories.

I water-ski and tried to wake-board.

I speak a foreign language

I have sold life insurance, annuities, stocks, bonds, health insurance, auto insurance, car insurance, cars, religion, ice cream, food, motorcycles, ATVs, magazines, long-distance telephone service, church raffle tickets, consulting services, supply-chain management software, massage machines, prescription drug card plans, men's and women's clothing.

I love people.

And there are several important techniques for learning to sell here:

1. Your ability to converse intelligently is in direct proportion to your life's experiences.

2. Your success in sales is directly proportional to things you find in common with your clients.

3. Selling anything helps you sell everything.

4. You have the possibility of making more sales while doing something you have in common with your client outside their office.

5. Most of your sales will happen because you love to sell and your customer loves to buy.

6. Beyond jokes and stories, if you are having fun in your life it will show in your career.

7. Never underestimate the capacity of your mind and your body.

8. Faith is universal.

9. No matter what your age, it is never too late to expand your life experiences.

**Life's most persistent and urgent question is,
'What are you doing for others'?**
- Martin Luther King

Chapter 10

Vinnie Bag-o-doughnuts is Alive and Well!

Unions have been my most interesting and entertaining clients.

I have had the pleasure of working with a number of them from the Boiler Makers in Palm Desert, California to the Masters, Mates and Pilots in Baltimore and hundreds of locals and nationals throughout the country.

In the spring of 2002 I was invited to be the keynote luncheon speaker for the Western Conference of Teamsters Leadership Meeting held in Honolulu. Those in attendance were all of the Presidents of the "Locals" West of the Mississippi. I shared the podium with Jimmy Hoffa, Jr. and later that week my wife and I joined he and his wife at the Polynesian Cultural Center on Oahu for a Luau.

We had a lot in common. Neither of us liked the Poi.

The interesting and provocative history of labor in our country is not to be discounted. Regardless of archaic stereotypes they have comprised and continue to position themselves as a significant buyer of products and services.

The pharmacy benefit management industry (PBM) had its nemeses in Labor. The International Ladies Garment Workers Union (IL-GWU) in New York City was the first entity to start a mail-order drug plan for their members. They pulled it together with a couple of local pharmacies that filled prescriptions and then mailed or delivered them to their union members. The members got their prescriptions for free (no co-pays) and the union had yet one more benefit for their rank and file. Later they incorporated prescription drug cards that could be used at retail pharmacies.

Selling to Unions was a cultural learning curve for me. But selling to them was no different than selling to Fortune 500 Companies, insurance companies or government entities. Just like all the others; they bid, shopped and bought. Like all of the others their bidding and buying styles covered a broad spectrum. Some Union Locals had total autonomy and others kicked all big decisions up to the regional, national or international headquarters. Sometimes national and international headquarters would endorse vendors that some locals would vote down.

Fortunately, prior to my career in the PBM industry I had a mentor that had been involved in labor issues for his entire career. Mr. Barton had been General Counsel to American Stores, one of the nation's largest grocery chains. Prior to that he had worked for the FBI and was a consultant between Unions and government during the McClellan Hearings more commonly known as the Velachi hearings chaired by Robert Kennedy in the early 1960's.

During the time I knew him Unions were not my target market. But he was retired and had a number of friends that had been officers with many Unions. I felt honored when he introduced me to them.

These were good and true men and women and I am happy to say that meeting them first hand when I was in my mid to late twenties gave me a life-long respect for them. I did not get involved in the politics, the undercurrent of controversy, or the reputed associations of some of them. They were just regular people who had difficult jobs in difficult times.

So it was with those memories that some ten years later I had the opportunity to start to sell to them. By then my mentor was old and frail. His union friends would not be of help to me because of their age. But I thought of them whenever meeting with Unions.

The United Auto Workers Union based in Detroit was a prime opportunity for us. I was introduced to them by my friend and business associate Lance who had sold a fifty million dollar program to Chrysler. In the late eighties and into the early nineties the UAW controlled all benefits for auto workers. Ultimately the manufacturers would have to sign-off on any benefit plan design changes. And many times these changes were subject to arbitration or union negotiation. Granted, the prescription drug plans we were selling were small potatoes compared to their other health care costs. But, as the most-used healthcare benefit, they knew it was imperative that the plan was designed and implemented successfully.

When Lance and I entered the scene Ford, GM, Chrysler, American Motors and Volkswagen of America controlled seventy percent of the automotive market in America and our little company only had just been awarded the Chrysler contract. For some other sales people this might have been a significant-enough victory. But I wasn't involved in that deal and wanted to get into the game.

Lance knew the people at the UAW so we decided to start there first. Again, we knew that the UAW would be a key player but we had a couple of significant hurdles, and each one was important.

First, we were young. I was thirty five and Lance was thirty. Unions at that time were being run by older men, who typically did business with older men. Lance had already worked through this with Chrysler so he had some valuable insight. We decided to bring in re-enforcements. Fortunately our Chief of Pharmacy, Jerry, was a likeable sixty-something, pipe-smoking South-Philly guy. Lance had used him when he sold Chrysler and we put him on our team for this strategy. The great thing about Jerry was that he loved to tell stories and he knew how to interweave pharmacy-speak. We would ask him to give a clinical over-view of the validity of disease management as it pertained to healthcare outcomes through pharmaceutical compliance and he would tell a story about a woman he used to fill prescriptions for when he had his own little neighborhood pharmacy. He took our older prospects back to times and places they had jointly shared long before Lance and I were born.

We could never do what he did.

But knowing that we needed him, and that he knew what he was talking about, kept us in the game and moved us up the pecking order of potential buyers.

The most commonly known fact of selling is that many potential buyers are empowered to say "no" and only a few are empowered to say "yes".

But finding those who can say "yes" is accomplished through using the "no's" as stepping stones.

With Jerry we were able to make the naysayers our friends, coaches and mentors to those who could say "yes".

Our friends at the UAW introduced us to the benefits team at American Motors then based in Toledo. By then Jerry was with us in every meeting. We set up the slide show, made the introductions and then turned the time over to the professor. This man was far too endearing and smart for anyone that had the power to say "yes" not to say "yes".

It turned out that Volkswagen of America was not fully unionized. We took Jerry with us, but they were a hip young crowd and Lance and I carried the day there. Jerry filled in the "pharma-speak". But our advantage there was in letting them know that by slightly tweaking the plan design, they could do an end run around the Unions with a plan that was perceived to be better.

These sales were significant at the time. But it was not until fifteen years later did I realize how significant.

When hired as Senior Vice President of Sales and Marketing for a company in Long Island one of my first mandates was to inventory our clients, evaluate their pricing models, compare and contrast them to what I knew of the competition and development a client retention campaign.

This is a big sentence for an even bigger job.

I discovered that our book of business was over sixty-five percent Union groups. I then found out that most of them had been on the books for five years or longer. They were very profitable customers, but their pricing was archaic. Indeed, a good competitor could step in and win more than half of them on price alone. Finally, and our most dangerous situation, was that we had written contracts with almost none of them. The files were full of letters of intent, correspondence confirming price, and description of plan design details. But no contracts.

This was further exacerbated by the fact that our little company had recently gone public and I knew that Board Members and stockholders alike would see this as a dangerous if not litigious position.

By my count we had close to forty different union accounts representing about two hundred million dollars in annual sales that did not have written contracts with us.

One of the biggest sales of my life was to develop a strategy to go out and re-sell an existing book of business and lower their price schedule without it appearing that we had been ripping them off.

Our CEO had only been onboard for about six months and had

spent most of that time taking the company public and trying to extricate my predecessor from her position. There is no way of describing how crippling senior staff compatibility issues can be on the growth of a company. But that is fodder for further books.

I knew he would not have given me this assignment had he not known that there was a problem.

After a day or two I asked him if we could go over my findings in a Senior Staff meeting, and he agreed.

He was a collaborator and an incredibly bright guy; close to genius level. But like most in that space he had some idiosyncrasies: liked walking around the corporate office in stocking feet, disliked wearing a neck tie but had a collection hung on his doorknob for when clients came to visit and lived with his wife and children on a sailboat throughout the year docked in Long Island Sound.

His business style was to delegate and collaborate. So it was no surprise that he agreed on a staff meeting.

When he hired me he also brought in a new VP of Operations and a new Chief Information Officer. The VP of Operations was from the Little Rock acquisition and looked talked and reasoned like Andy Griffin. The CIO was without question the most intelligent person I have ever met or worked with in any capacity. She had an MBA from Columbia and a Doctorate of information Technology from NYU. Of course I would want these people in any meeting with me.

I laid out the results of my inventory.

In her pragmatic way the CIO came right to the point.

"It sounds like we need to go offer all of these clients a contract with lower prices. They sign and they get the good price." For her, everything had a logical box. Brilliant!

Andy, from Little Rock, was far more contemplative, and in his sweet southern executive-speak he turned to me and said, "Good job Jim, let me know if I can help."

The CEO got a smile on his face and turned to me. We had all learned that he loved to create situations that polarized us, forcing us to take a stand even if it was as simple as asking for help.

I was the only one in the room that had Union experience and they knew it. At the age of forty-eight I was also the oldest in the room. And I had been in the PBM business longer than any of them.

"Do any of us know these accounts?" I asked.

"Nope." said the CEO.

"Who sold these accounts?" I continued to prod.

"The woman you replaced." He Answered, full well knowing that this was going to make things even harder.

"And they loved her." He threw more gas on the fire.

Ironically I had worked with this woman some fifteen years before and my success had garnered her respect but she was extremely competitive. Her envy of my successes was palatable. So we weren't exactly buddies. The thought of calling her to ask for help was a fleeting fantasy.

She was also suing us for firing her.

Glad I wasn't in on that.

"So I would like to propose a plan." I announced.

They were a little shocked that I was so prepared, but these meetings were like playing executive "Jeopardy". We knew the categories, but the questions and answers were up to each individual contestant.

"We are going to put together an Advisory Board." I announced. "Each of these non-contracted clients and a few select others will be invited to participate. The mandate of this Board will be to help us formulate product development and re-pricing strategies. In the process we will wine and dine them, come to a group-consensus on price and by the time we are through this process they will be anxious to lock themselves into multi-year contracts. Those who cannot participate will be approached with the group propositions and the opportunity to execute contracts with a provision that they have an open invitation to join the Board at the next meeting."

I turned to Andy. "I will need a mind-sizzling power-point that leads them to forgone conclusions about what you are doing to improve Best Practices."

To the CIO I said, "I want you to put together about ten slides that will spin their brains backwards about your vision for making our company an industry innovator in technology."

I turned to the CEO, "I would like to plan for a mid-morning meeting, an afternoon golf outing and a dinner.

My best guess is that we will spend about ten thousand dollars. And you will need to get the Chairman of the Board to make an appearance, and say a few words about how we are an 'open shop' and interested in Unionizing our non-exempt employees."

The CEO responded, "Get me a couple of potential dates and we will make it happen." He was ecstatic.

There is nothing like experience to increase confidence.

Six years prior to this, while working for another vendor we had faced a crisis. Five new classes of drugs were being flooded by medications recently approved by the FDA. You might remember some of these: Prozac, Lipitor, Viagra, oral drugs for migraines, and new drugs for hypertension and indigestion. With the introduction of these drugs we knew that our client's aggregate drug costs were going to escalate anywhere from fifteen to thirty percent. So we called the biggest ones in and formed an Advisory Counsel. In essence we were giving them a heads up by asking them to help us help them.

It had worked then, and I knew it would work now.

But there was one more element I knew I needed for my Union friends. I needed some gray hair on the podium. So I went through every department and regardless of their job description I identified our oldest employees, got permission from their supervisors and tapped each of them for a short presentation.

It was miraculous. We found gold among the "silver" in our cubicles. People that had been with the company for years who had been hired to do clinical, technology, or customer service jobs were honored to step up and share their wisdom and insight.

We had about twenty clients participate on the Union Advisory Board, more attended the golf outing and we invited spouses to join them at the dinner.

We gave plaques to each of them and asked them to display them in their offices. The recognition part was obvious, but we also wanted potential competitors to see that they were calling on very special clients of ours.

Plaques were also presented to the employees that participated in the presentations.

We used this as a template for other vertical markets. Same design, different content.

This was "sales" at its best.

Sometimes you divide and conquer and sometimes you combine and win.

By the end of the day we had reduced our margins on this segment of our business. But, when it came time to present them with annual savings reports we won them over again and were able to add additional products and services for additional fees.

They loved us and felt like they were part of the solution.

They also became incredible references and opened doors to several more accounts.

———————————

Of all the vertical markets; Union buyers love golf and food more than any other. And usually they have several golf and dinner events every year. You might be asked to contribute to the charities they sponsor, but these contributions are well worth the expense and it makes working with them a whole lot of fun. They also have annual raffles. Donating and bidding at these raffles is a great way to brand you and your company.

Following are excellent techniques you should have learned from this chapter to learn to sell:

1. Every target market has an opening

2. If you aren't the person to make the sale, bring in the person who will

3. Make your customers your brain trust

4. Do not be afraid to repeat success

5. Sharing the sales process means you have people to celebrate with.

I don't believe people are looking for the meaning of life as much as looking for the experience of being alive.
- Joseph Campbell, author of the classic <u>The Power of Myth</u>.

Chapter 11

Sex Sells

> **Think of all the beauty**
> **still left around you**
> **and be happy.**
> *- Anne Frank*

The strengths of men and women are not mutually exclusive. For those of us that have lived a half a century or more and been selling for over three decades we know that the opportunities for success in "sales" are available to everyone. The potential here is as expansive as a person's imagination.

When I am going after sales of any size I always look for help and I want the best person for the job to help me.

And so does the buyer.

The challenge is to make the point while avoiding the reaction.

One of my good friends teaches graduate business courses. She also teaches diversity training and diversity marketing. And obviously, knowing the difference is no different than knowing the difference between which customers want vanilla and which want chocolate, strawberry, or butter-pecan.

As I am writing this book I am watching Paul McCartney singing "I Saw her Standing There" on the Grammy Awards. I heard him sing it on the Ed Sullivan Show in 1962. Most of the people in the audience at the 2009 Grammy Awards could be our grandchildren...and they are going nuts for his music just like I was forty-five years ago.

Classics remain classic.

Classic sales techniques are the same.

Learning to sell is something that works forever.

So this begs the question: who is the best person for the job?

You have already read how about "Influence Marketing" and through using it how to get clients all over the country. You also have read how to team up with people older and wiser in order to meet the needs of clients. You have also learned how working with so-called "minority contractors" can help win huge accounts.

I am the first to admit that I never closed a sale without the help of many who had different and better skill sets than mine.

When I stepped from direct sales into sales management the first strategy I deployed was to provide every sales executive with a "collaborative" team.   I also opened the gates for them to have access to everyone in the company. From the CEO to the IT Techs, I made sure that if we had a resource to close a sale it would be made available.

But there is some additional information that affirms the power of collaborative selling.

Sex sells! But not the way it does on TV.

When I worked with the City of Baltimore it was my first opportunity to try to obtain the business of an all African American client. From Mayor Schmoke to the clerks in the Benefits Department, they were all African Americans. So it is true. A white kid raised in Utah can grow up to sell a half-billion dollar account to them. Yes, I was the Mitt Romney of my time. Out of place, but not intimidated. But I didn't do it alone.

To win that sale did I think about bringing in a Black co-worker? Sure I did. But I didn't have any Black co-workers.

The Director of Benefits for the City was a very bright woman. To win that sale did I think about bringing in a woman? Sure I did. But I didn't call the home office and ask for a woman to help me.

To get the help I needed I wrote up a job description for an Account Manager that would help with the sale and then manage the account if we won it. I gave the request to our VP of Account Services and he made the decision.

He appointed the best Account Manager for the job. Not because she was a woman. But he appointed her because she had the best clinical and cross-departmental skills on our team. After all, this would be our largest account and it would be incredibly difficult to manage.

I simply wanted the best person for the job. And together we were.

The first large company I worked for and the companies I worked for in White Plains and on Long Island were all owned and operated by Jewish people. For some reason they thought I was the best person for the job when they hired me. And it turned out they were right.

And here is a "shocker" that will probably be quoted out of context: I have always believed that women make the best sales people. And I know that many of my clients have the same opinion.

So, how did I use this information to help me make sales?

With few exceptions I always asked our top women to join me with finalist presentations.

And here is another glaring generality about sales people. If you are a man don't envy your female peers, partner with them.

Women also are excellent collaborators.

This is not a "sexist" issue. It is a "sales success" issue.

If you are a man who wants to move forward toward a successful selling career, I recommend that you get a female mentor, strategic partner or consultant.

If you are a woman who wants to move forward toward a successful selling career, I recommend that you get a male mentor, strategic partner or consultant.

If your boss is a woman you are very fortunate.

Sex sells!

Shortly after winning the State of Montana contract and the Montana Healthcare Coalition which included Montana University System, First interstate Bank of Montana, Montana Power and the Montana Builder's Association I also won the State of Wyoming. Then I won the largest School District in Utah, Marriott Corporation based in Maryland and PEPCO, the power company for Washington DC. And of course I still had the City of Baltimore and a number of other accounts.

I needed help and asked my boss if I could have the best Account Manager available out of our Phoenix operation for the Western Accounts. And he gave me the best.

After several years and hundreds of accounts I was talking to one of my peers. She was an incredibly successful woman whose territory was the tough Northeastern US. She had won our annual sales contest five years in a row. I asked her if she could define her secret to sales success. Her response was astonishing. "The VP of Account Services has consistently assigned me the best men on his team."

"Men?" I asked.

"Sure." She replied. "These guys are great."

"But wait, all my account managers are women." I responded.

It was an epiphany.

"And that is why it only took you two years to catch up and beat me out of the national sales award." She smiled.

I called the VP of Account Services and told him what I had just figured out.

"Sex sells." He said.

And I knew what he meant.

———————

Not long after this I received a call from a broker I had been working with out of Salt Lake City. He had walked me into the largest school district in the State of Utah the previous year and we had won the account away from a viable incumbent.

"Jim, don't know if this will mean a sale but the Health and Welfare Fund of Utah has asked me to find them some help."

"What's going on?" I asked.

"They are being hammered with filling claims for Prozac and need some advice."

Prozac had hit the market a year before and it's manufacturer had made a bold strategic decision. The drug was approved for those with mild or episodic depression. But instead of marketing it to psychiatrists or other mental health professionals they sent their detail reps to general practitioners and OBGYN docs. Prior to Prozac the anti-depressant drugs of choice were Valium, Ativan and other sedatives. Prozac was not chemically addictive and had exponentially found acceptance. The book "Listening to Prozac" by Peter D. Kramer had become a best seller and if you weren't on the drug you wanted to ask your physician why not!

Basically many people needed help for depression but did not want to go to a "talk-therapist". The drug was a blockbuster.

I had reams of utilization data from other large groups and called my Account Manager and asked her for suggestions and to join me for the meeting in Utah.

She replied, "I will have the clinical department run a query on utilization for our entire data base to identify demographics. I have some ideas."

When we got to Utah and sat down with the State Medicaid committee I turned the meeting over to my Account Manager. She let the State tell us that their total drug claims had increased by twenty percent in number of prescriptions and over thirty percent in actual costs just as a result of Prozac.

Then my Account Manager told them the facts that came from her in far better form than they would have from me.

"Assuming your claimants are reflective of national trends, over eighty-five percent of your Prozac users are women." There was a collective gasp. "And they are using the drug not just for episodic depression, but for a number of off-label uses that include: menstrual anxiety, ADD, ADHD, geriatric agitation, OCD, panic disorder and weight control."

While the committee was comprised of both men and women, it was important that a woman present this information. The facts would have been no different had I presented them, but it was an example of the effectiveness of using the right "sex to sell" a concept.

After our meeting, the State of Utah decided to try putting the drug on prior authorization. This required physicians to give definitive medical reasons for prescribing Prozac. The State set up a call-center to take the calls. It was to no avail. The call center "server" went down within the first week due to the huge number of calls.

This story is only a vehicle to help you understand that the strengths of each sex is what makes "sex sell". And here are the sales techniques from this chapter:

1. Selling is always collaborative

2. Sex Sells

3. Skill always trumps race

4. If you are a man, get over it

5. Get the right person for the job

To dare, is to lose one's footing momentarily.
To not dare is to lose oneself.
- Soren Kierkegaard, Philosopher and Theologian

Chapter 12

Friends and Family

To love and win is the best thing.
To love and lose, the next best.
- William M. Thackeray, novelist

I have over sixty first cousins and with the majority of them married with kids and grand kids it makes for a pretty big family.

We were all raised on or near farms, had weekly or monthly family get-togethers and for those few who lived a day's drive away, we planned most family vacations around seeing them.

May not be the same as your situation, but like everyone, I came from somewhere.

Several years into my sales career I decided that I wanted to get back in touch with all my relatives. So I published a family newsletter. Over the years we had exchanged Christmas Cards, and many of them included annual news updates. But we really were drifting further and further apart. We were no longer connected by a common thread of agronomy and geography. We were spread all over the country in a variety of occupations.

For my first newsletter I called my three siblings and asked for an update on their families and then I filled in the blanks with information about our parents and also included a short professional biography about myself. I also encouraged family members to send me news and articles. My first mailing went to over a hundred family members.

A week later I received a phone call from a cousin I hadn't seen in over fifteen years.

"James?" He asked. (My family and friends call me James). "Guess who this is?" I had no idea.

"I have no idea." I replied.

"It is your cousin Paul."

"No way!" I replied.

"Way!" He responded.

"Hey, I got your newsletter. What a fantastic idea. I am already looking forward to the next one."

The family newsletter idea was already worth the effort. Just reconnecting with Paul alone would be worth it.

We talked about a number of things and then the conversation took an interesting turn.

"James, as you know I am living in Rockville, Maryland. But what you probably don't know is that I am a Colonel with the Army and my current assignment is Assistant Director at Walter Reed Medical Center."

"Sounds great," I said. "Last I heard you were on assignment in Central American with a team of fifty peace-makers fighting the contras." My information was sketchy.

"True." He said. "Six months of hell in the jungle. But we all came back alive."

Everyone in the military is a hero to me.

Paul went on, "But now I have a new assignment and after reading your newsletter I think we might need to spend some time together."

"Sounds great. What do you have in mind?"

"I have been assigned to deploy an initial memorandum for a Statement of Work for the Department of Defense. They want to investigate the possibility of contracting for mail-service prescriptions for all U.S. based military. We call it Tri-care."

"Where do we start?" I asked.

"First things first." He said.

"How about coming down to Walter Reed and we put together a strategy. This is really an intelligence gathering assignment. So until I know more about your industry I can't tell where to go with what you have."

"Perfect."

We set a time and within a week I was at Walter Reed. At the time I had several large accounts and prospects in the Washington D.C./ Baltimore corridor and knew the turf. But the closest I had been to the military was working as a "dead" extra in a war movie filmed near my home town when I was a teenager.

Paul and I went through everything I knew about the mail-service drug industry. I also brought about a hundred slides, brochures and a few proposals we had recently issued.

It was a full-day working meeting and near the end of it he invited in his superior. At that point I let him reiterate what he had learned. He was a quick study and his boss absorbed it quickly.

Afterward Paul told me that they would need a few days to sort through the material and then he would get back to me.

When he called back he had extraordinary news.

"James, we have decided to convene an executive session to have you go through everything you discussed with me. We just need to know which of two dates would work for you."

I had one of them free.

"That's great," he said. "Here is the strategy: there will be Four Star Generals from each of the military branches. Navy, Army, Air force and Marines will be represented, plus an aid to each, and we are waiting for a confirmation from the National Guard. The meeting will be held in the Eisenhower Library and start promptly at nine-hundred hours. We will work for three hours, mess will be served in the room and then the meeting will be open to Q and A. We are still considering this a working group so we are not looking for a sales presentation."

I was stunned.

"If this plays out, how big of a program would this be? I asked.

"The US bases are divided into three regions." He said. "Each region has about a million members including family. Then there is the Veteran's Administration which nationwide covers about ten million."

He paused while I caught my breath.

"Most likely a beta test would be done with one of them first. But remember. This is the DOD. They do not work fast and they always go out to bid with an SOW."

So far Paul had been protecting me from too many military acronyms, but they we starting to seep into his speech.

I did a quick mental calculation. Not counting the VA any one region would be about two hundred million in prescription claims.

"Sounds like we have a plan." I confirmed. "I will be in your office at eight-thirty."

I arrived on time wearing my most conservative suit, crisply starched shirt with small gold cuff links matching my watch, yellow silk tie, white starched pocket handkerchief and shoes shined to maximum luster. I had never served in the military, but I knew the expectations.

Paul and I went to the room first and as we entered he explained to me that the Eisenhower Library was adjacent to the Eisenhower living quarters where President Eisenhower had spent his last days. The room was set up with a "U" shaped table with a projection screen in place at the open end. I set up and tested my video presentation and just as I finished the Generals started to file in.

They were in their "best-dress" regalia, but were congenial to each other and obviously comfortable in working together. I had wondered who would solute who. But there was mostly handshakes and back-slapping. They were joined by the Senior Officers at Walter Reed.

Paul introduced me to each of them before we sat down and when he called the meeting together he introduced me to the group. As a part of full disclosure he also told them of our relationship and how as kids we had milked cows, caught frogs and raised as much hell as two Mormon boys could together. That drew a chuckle and it was obvious that they were open to our home-spun up-bringing.

My presentation went well. I knew my stuff well enough to move forward without script or notes and the three hours flew buy.

"Mess" was served and in the interest of time the Q&A started before we finished the excellent meal.

Since the subject matter was relatively new to my audience the questions had more to do with deployment strategies.

This was very cool.

Although I was careful to respond to their questions with, "Sir, yes sir." Instead of saying, "Cool question."

I had never discussed "deployment strategies" with real military brass before. This was also very cool.

When the meeting was over each General came to me personally and thanked me for my time and the "intelligence" I had provided them. I was honored to be there and still consider this to be one of the most memorable experiences of my sales career.

After the "brass" left, Paul and his CO thanked me also and told me that it would probably be a month before a next step.

Paul and I stayed in touch informally, but about a month later he asked me to come back to Walter Reed.

"The combined 'Brass' were very impressed with your presentation and their aids have vetted your information to their complete satisfaction. The next step is for us to write a Statement of Work (SOW) and breaking normal procedure they have asked me to ask you if you would help us."

"Absolutely" I replied.

"Just so we are clear," he said. "We are also hopeful that you and your firm bid on the business. So in order to build a fire-wall between the writing of the SOW and the actual bid process we have asked a military contractor to step in. You will work with him to construct the SOW, but he will actually present it to us. He knows how these instruments are written, but of course he has no clue as to the practices and procedures of your industry."

"Works for me."

I was anxious to learn more about the bidding process of the military and once again was presented with the opportunity to take my sales experience to a totally new environment.

I might add here that up until this point I had kept my boss out of the loop. I had considered my relationship with my cousin sacrosanct and until I knew that there was really a sales opportunity available I wanted to keep this one close to the vest.

My boss was a good guy. But he couldn't sell. Coincidentally my fellow sales executives used to joke behind his back that he couldn't give away USO dance tickets on a troop train.

Now here I was, holding the USO dance tickets and getting ready to board the troop train.

But, since the SOW was now in the hands of the Consultant and the potential for sales errors were off the table I decided to share my experiences with my boss.

He was stunned and pleased. Of course he was used to similar conversations with me. Many of them went like this:

"Where are you this week?" he asked in a friendly hopeful way. I always had good news for him. Though sometimes it was "alarmingly-good".

"San Juan." I replied

"You mean Puerto Rico!" He exclaimed.

His voice was neither inquisitive nor friendly.

"Do you realize what the BOSS will say when he finds out?"

By now he was screaming into the phone.

I waited for a few seconds and then replied. "Maybe you better start the conversation by telling him that I just made a presentation to Blue Shield of Puerto Rico and they are very interested."

The phone was silent.

"Why do I even ask?" He mumbled.

Then he said, "What do you need from us to get the deal done?"

"Just give Jerry (our Senior Director of Pharmacy) to buy some suntan lotion. We will probably need to make a trip together back here in a couple of weeks."

"How big is Blue Shield of Puerto Rico?" He asked.

"Well, just so you know, they call it Triple S down here and they are basically the only insurer on the Island. They have about a million members. Potentially a two hundred million dollar account."

He was stunned, and probably not knowing what else to ask, he asked me how much a plane ticket from Philadelphia to Puerto Rico cost me.

"Less than a ticket to Cleveland" I responded.

"Good answer." He said.

Since my success with the company had been so rapid I had been given a long leash and usually didn't need to let anyone know where I was going to be. I just called in the victories. And this was another one.

But back to the DOD SOW.

It was time to come clean on this one.

After talking to the boss we decided to bring the Military Contractor/Consultant to our offices in Philadelphia where we would craft the SOW with the help of all senior staff members. Our objective was to present a fair document, but nevertheless one that had some of our unique capabilities imbedded in the small print.

My cousin Paul was right about the slow process of the government.

The SOW was finally released a year later. By then I had been recruited to be Senior Vice President of Sales for another company and knowing what I knew about how the SOW was written I recommended that my new employer decline to bid.

As expected, the company that I had worked for when we wrote the SOW won the contract. The contract was so big that it buried the company. The stress of trying to keep the account happy and the company from failing caused my replacement to have a fatal heart attack. He was a good man and yet another fatality of corporate life. The DOD contract eventually brought the company to its knees and it was forced to accept a buy-out offer from a competitor.

Once again, this was not a sale for me. But it was a singular event in an incredible career and carried with it several important sales lessons.

1. Always let your family and friends know what you sell and why you sell it.

2. Never underestimate the help of family and friends. They may be in places you could never go on your own.

3. Where you came from is who you are and most people came from similar places. Let them know.

4. Know when to use your boss and when not to.

5. Even Four Star Generals buy things

> **The world is a dangerous place,**
> **not because of those who do evil,**
> **but because of those who look on and do nothing.**
> *- Albert Einstein*

Chapter 13

Smartest Guy in the Room

**I am always doing that which I cannot,
in order that I may learn how to do it.**
- Pablo Picasso

After almost three decades in the pharmaceutical business I still only know how to pronounce and spell about a dozen drugs. I also only know about ten major diseases or common maladies. My degree is a B.A. in Communications with Major studies in Advertising and minor studies in Japanese.

I almost never considered myself the "smartest guy in the room."

At every job I ever held, both in sales and other fields my peers were always smarter than me.

But I refuse to be intimidated by my ignorance.

I was once recruited from a sales position with a life insurance company to be a Loss Control Engineer for a fire protection engineering company.

"Jim." A man approached me after a church meeting we had both just attended. "Do you have an engineering background?"

"I don't really like trains much." I replied with a smile on my face.

"Here is my card." He said. "Can you stop by my office tomorrow afternoon?"

"Sure." I said as I tried to decipher all the letters after his name and absorb the meaning of his title which was "Manager, Fire Protection and Hydraulic Engineering".

I didn't know what "Hydraulic Engineering" was, but I did by the time I met with him. Being a "quick-study" is a sales secret.

"We want to enhance our engineering staff with people that have unique sales skills." He said after we sat down in his office on the twentieth story of the First Pennsylvania Bank Building overlooking Independence Mall in Philadelphia.

"I guess you better tell me more." I replied.

"What we do here is simple. Highly technical. But simple. We do fire protection engineering for our parent company. It insures some of the largest corporations and structures in the country. This means that we make sure that the buildings, equipment, processes and infrastructures meet all of the fire codes necessary to protect them against loss from fire." He could see that I was keeping up so he continued.

"In order to do this we hire employees that have college degrees in engineering. Specifically we try to hire hydraulic engineers because much of what we do is to design and re-design sprinkler and other fire suppression systems. To keep consistency in our projects we send these engineers to our own school in Worcester, Massachusetts every six months for three week training sessions."

I was wondering why he asked me to meet with him. So I asked him.

"Why did you want to meet with me?"

"Pretty simple." He said. "These engineers are technical professionals. But when it comes time to convince a CFO that in order to protect a plant and avoid increasing insurance premiums the company would have to spend a couple of million dollars."

He went on.

"I have known you for about a year and noticed that you are good on your feet and a quick study. I would like to offer you a position with our company, send you to our engineering school and use you as a model for future recruiting."

By that time in my career I had put myself through college selling life insurance to other college students. Then after college had continued to sell insurance, also worked in a men's clothing store and two nights a week I worked in a telemarketing firm selling magazines.

Paying the price to learn how to sell can come from many different ways.

I wasn't the smartest guy in the room and hadn't been the smartest guy on campus. But while my fellow students were studying I was learning to sell and working as a Master of Ceremonies for a college variety show.

While listening to my friend in his office I was thinking about one thing. At the young age of nineteen, I had gone to Japan and learned to speak Japanese.

So I thought to myself, "If I could learn Japanese, then I could learn anything."

So I took the job and off I went to Worcester, Massachusetts to learn how to figure out how much water pressure needs to enter a sprinkler system in a basement in order for it to put out a fire on the twentieth floor. Then if there wasn't enough pressure I had to learn how to calculate what had to be done to make enough pressure, figure out how much that would cost, and then convince a CFO that he should spend the money.

I was the only non-engineer in the class and definitely not the smartest guy in the room. But I passed the course and spent the next four years doing what I had been taught to do.

This experience was a template for future "learning curve" opportunities in sales.

Some two decades later I was invited to speak to a physician conference in Michigan. The conference was sponsored by one of the larger HMOs in the State of Michigan and I had been assigned to speak on the topic: "Prescribing Patterns for Disease Management and Aggregate Outcomes".

The audience was comprised of about three hundred physicians of all specialties. Every one of them had unique qualifications, extraordinary academy credentials, year's of practical experience and was WAY smarter than me.

But I had been asked to speak to them, by one of them. He was the Chief Medical Officer of the HMO. It was apparent that he was impressed enough with what he had learned from me as one of my clients that he wanted all of his peers to learn the same.

The truth of the matter is, that I knew what I knew after many years of looking at global data trends that had been compiled by physicians, MBA's, pharmacists, and analysts who had been my support team members. These are people who individually had contributed information for an aggregate sum of information that I was fortunate to collate. It was not my information. It was neither unique nor proprietary. But I had been there as it evolved and observed the impact of new drugs entering the market, generic drugs being approved and a myriad of other changes to the pharmaceutical healthcare landscape.

About a year before this speaking engagement I had been given the opportunity to meet with the Senior Officers of a Medicare HMO in Baltimore. I had actually been referred to them by my friends at The City of Baltimore.

When I arrived at the meeting I was surprised to find that two of the four executive officers were physicians. Like most of my first-call appointments I had positioned myself in front of them with nothing more than my notepad. And in this situation I was indeed glad that I did.

At that time there were a number of small insurance companies that had been given Federal equivalency premiums to administer Medicare programs for qualified individuals. This was long before Medicare Part D came on the horizon. But this Baltimore-based plan had determined that they could incorporate a prescription drug component and keep their total budget within the Federal guidelines.

Within minutes of the start of this meeting it was obvious that the physicians who ran the company had compiled a formulary of drugs that they felt could be included. They then continued to ask questions about my company's capabilities to screen and authorize these drugs in accordance with disease management protocols.

I was in over my head. And I told them.

Not that curtly, but I told them that I would like to bring in our Directory of Pharmacy and our Chief Medical Officer.

Two weeks later we were back and I had prepped my medical staff with the issues that had been presented in the original meeting.

In the meantime a competitor had entered the equation. But they had made a tactical error. In their first meeting they had conducted a full-blown sales presentation.

We were awarded the contract without ever making a sales presentation.

But, after the contract was awarded, I asked them if I could come in for a training session. It was my sales presentation. But I had learned that clients who bought based on a single buying factor without knowing the breadth of capacities available to them usually experienced operational problems.

As I went through the training session we had the opportunity to discuss, review and implement additional products and procedures that they otherwise had not learned. This forced a thirty-day delay on our implementation. But the advantages of this post-sales training avoided numerous potential pitfalls.

At another point in my career I was invited by a professor at the University of Pennsylvania to speak to their graduate healthcare administration students at the Wharton School of Business.

After my one-hour lecture concluded the Dean of the Health Administration Department stood and asked if it was possible for me to remain at the podium for the second hour of their class for a Q and A session. There were about a hundred and fifty students in the class, all of whom were working on Masters and Doctorate Degrees.

I wasn't the smartest guy in the room. But they thought I was.

The extraordinary knowledge of my buyers is constantly superseded by administrative and organizational blind spots. Unveiling these blind spots to my customers has been the key to making sales.

Techniques learned from knowing you are not the smartest guy in the room are huge advantages in making sales:

1. If you have ever learned anything, you can learn more

2. Refuse to be intimidated by your ignorance

3. Know when you don't know something and bring in the experts

4. Do not underestimate what your client does not know

5. At some point in the sales process make sure that your client hears all of your company's capabilities

Chapter 14

Never Make a Cold Call

When I finished college I wasn't offered a big job. I had blown through college in three years by taking the minimum number of credits they would allow. During that time I got married, and took a job selling life insurance to other college students. This also included two weeks of sales training at a "sales institute" for the insurance company I worked for.

I still remember some of the things I learned during those two weeks and they have helped me throughout my sales career.

The most important thing I learned was to use my client's name every time I address them.

I also learned how to sell over the phone. After college I used this training to work as a part-time telemarketer.

I still use the technique of using my client's names every time I address them.

But I decided a long time ago that neither telemarketing nor cold-calling were my strong points.

I avoid rejection at all costs.

But avoiding rejection in a sales career takes incredible creativity and ingenuity.

About five years ago I accepted a position with a company that had been unsuccessful in breaking into the California market. I had always wanted to live on the beach so I accepted the position, bought a Mustang convertible and asked them for a list of prospects.

This company had hired me because I had started an audit company, audited one of their larger customers and found over twenty-five million dollars in overcharges. I sold off my company and was looking for my next opportunity when a head-hunter called me and told me he had a job offer for me that was designed to get me out of the market and required that I sign a two-year non-compete. He also said that I probably would be fired within six months of being hired.

I love a challenge.

And like I said, I always wanted to live at the beach, so I took the job with the strings attached.

They sent me a prospect list that included over two thousand prospects from Anchorage to San Diego and East to Salt Lake City and South to Phoenix. All of these prospects had been called on unsuccessfully by others assigned to this territory. Only a few had become customers and they had become disillusioned and cancelled their contracts. Basically I was hired to fail. But I knew it and so did my employer.

I had names, addresses, phone numbers and cryptic notations. The average size of these prospects was under fifty-thousand dollars in potential revenue.

Not my market, not my first choice.

But I had found a place on Lido Isle in Newport Harbor in Newport Beach and I already had my convertible top down and decided that my air-travel days were over. I wanted to spend some serious time on the Pacific Coast Highway.

Wanting to avoid the inevitable rejection in this sales situation, I made a call.

I called my good friend Owen.

"This is Owen." He replied.

"Hey buddy, its Jim. I know you are retired, but I've got some work for you."

"Great!" he said. "Want me to start today or tomorrow."

Owen was the master of the "either-or" close. And manipulated the "assumed consent" close better than anyone I had ever known.

But most important, he is the master of all masters on the phone.

I had hired him a few years early when I was running a national sales force, and had known him for almost twenty years.

When working for me he always had more appointments than anyone on my team.

For him, the telephone was a money machine.

"I've got over two thousand prospects in twenty cities and I need you to set up the appointments."

"Same business as before?"

"Yup."

"Got some sales literature for me?"

"Hard copies are in the mail and I'm putting the web-site in an e-mail to you."

"Great. What about the list?"

"E-mail attachment."

"Where do you want to go first?"

"How about San Francisco starting after lunch next Monday? I'm driving up this weekend. Then I will either stay there all week or you can go ahead and schedule stuff for me driving back down the coast."

"What's the deal?"

"How about twenty bucks for every appointment you schedule and twenty bucks more if it holds. I'll send you a check every Saturday."

"These are just meet-and-greets right?" Owen confirmed.

"You know me." I said. "But my golf clubs will be in the trunk if anyone wants to play."

"How about lunches or dinners?"

"Absolutely."

"Can I just e-mail you the appointments as I get them?"

"Sure." I said. "I will have my Blackberry with me at the beach."

"Sweet."

Owen lives in Florida, but we didn't even talk about the time differences. He is a smart guy.

Over the next three months I met about four hundred of the prospects on the list.

In one of our weekly sales calls my boss had actually congratulated me on the number of sales calls I had been making each week and asked the other sales people what they needed to keep up with me. One of them suggested that corporate may want to hire a telemarketer to schedule appointments.

My boss responded that getting someone who could screen and qualify calls in our highly technical business was virtually impossible.

My boss had only been in the business for a year. And I hadn't told him about Owen.

It was late fall and most clients had already renewed their contracts with their existing vendors for the new calendar year. But I learned what they needed. They needed education. And more specifically they all had to obtain at least ten Continuing Education Credits each year in order to maintain their licenses.

I contacted the State of California Insurance Department, provided it with my CV and a one-hour lesson plan. They appointed me as a Certified Continuing Education Teacher.

"Owen." I called him on my blackberry from the beach.

"What's going on?" He asked.

"Got a new script for you and some new prospects."

"Great, what are we doing now?"

"I have sent you a list of the officers of each chapter of the Health Underwriters Association. Give them a call and let them know that I am certified as a CE instructor and would be available speak at one of their luncheons at no charge. They hold them monthly. I have also sent you a class outline and you know the rest."

"You are a smart guy." he said. "This should be fun."

And it was.

Over the next four months I accepted ten speaking engagements ranging from twenty to two hundred in attendance. I was not allowed to make a sales presentation, or include my corporate logo on my power-points. But "table favors" were allowed and so I provided each attendee with a gift bag that had a business card, a bag of chocolate and a coupon worth a free lunch with me at the restaurant of their choice.

And then my phone started to ring.

I got two types of calls.

The best were from those who had attended the luncheons and they were calling to invite me to take them to lunch and meet their people.

The other was from my boss.

He wasn't happy.

It seems that my peers in other parts of the company had been trying to hold "prospect seminars". They had been sending out invitations, renting large hotel conference rooms and flying in home-office executives. But at best, they were only getting five or six prospects to show up to their five-thousand dollar business parties.

I had been e-mailing my trip reports and he finally was getting around to reading them.

Why was he angry?

My idea was working and his wasn't.

I had made presentations to almost two-thousand people at virtually no cost to the company.

I told him that he was welcome to plagiarize my strategy.

He was not amused.

He asked for a copy of my power-point and he wanted me to stay on the phone until he received and reviewed it.

I e-mailed it to him.

He hated it because it did not have our corporate logo on it.

I told him why.

He didn't care.

He fired me.

The job had lasted seven months. This was a month longer than the head-hunter had warned. I knew I was doomed. But I also knew what I was doing. My boss had only been in the business for a year. I had been in the business for twenty-three years. Owen had been in it for three years.

This chapter was written for sales managers and the strategies are obvious:

1. Never underestimate the ambition of your salespeople

2. Hiring experienced sales people has two advantages: what they can do and what they can do for you, don't waste either advantage

3. Good telemarketers are worth every penny you pay them

4. Being good at what you do is not necessarily appreciated by everyone

5. Get to know your industry's trade groups and invite yourself to speak to them

**If you don't learn from your mistakes,
there's no sense making them.**
- Anonymous

Chapter 15

The Gray-matter Close

Great spirits have always
encountered violent opposition
from mediocre minds.
- Albert Einstein

"What is this?" I asked.

Dan, one of our Customer Service Representatives, had walked into my office and handed me a DVD shaped like a flat tire tread.

"It's a DVD shaped like a flat tire tread." He said with a smile. "You know. It goes along with our pit-crew theme. Go on. Pop it in your laptop."

"I did and up popped a simulation of our web-site and an interactive video of our client reporting software."

"This is totally sick!" I replied.

"Knew you would like it" He said in his Long Island accent. "Check this out." He grabbed my mouse and clicked on some other buttons.

Up popped a video of our recent trade show where our booth was crammed with people trying to get a turn at our NASCAR slot-car race set. And there I was with a couple of our sales people. We were all decked out in our NASCAR jackets and caps with our corporate logo. It looked like we were trying to control a buying frenzy for our products.

"Did I say this is totally sick!" I exclaimed.

"...thought this might be a great insert for the new marketing packets." He said, knowing I was totally jacked.

"Can I keep this one?" I asked as I stuck it in my shirt pocket.

"I can burn a bunch and also print and attach cover labels."

"Why aren't you working for me?" I asked.

"You never asked." He replied with a smile.

"Ask your Manager to come and see me and then go make me about ten of these."

"Thanks boss." He said as he left my office.

Dan is one of a kind. I never asked him how he had ended up in our Customer Service Department because once he was on my staff we were way too busy challenging each other with hi-tech sales ideas. It was a constant battle to keep him away from our CIO who also wanted him. But he was a self-taught study in sales acumen and had no place in the IT department.

He was a sales guy.

The cool thing was that Dan wasn't a nerd. Quite the opposite, he played golf, flew airplanes and was a great story teller. After a couple months in my marketing department I made him a Sales Executive. I needed him to help us with Unions and the other New York City and north Jersey markets.

As a native Long Islander he was a perfect fit and his technical knowledge gave him that edge that New York buyers look for in a sales exec.

I learned a bunch of sales lessons from this rookie salesman.

Within a few short months of getting him on my team he landed us the opportunity to bid on Empire Blue Cross, the Blue Cross plan for New York City.

As with most other very large groups they had sent us an enormous RFP and it took two of my proposal writers three full weeks to get it together.

Dan got a call a week after submitting our bid and ran in to my office where he put it on speaker.

"You have been chosen as one of three finalists.

"Why?" Dan asked. (He pretty much always said what I would have said.) "And I've got you on speaker in my boss's office so make it good."

Dan was unabashed New York through and through.

"Glad to meet you I said."

The caller returned my pleasantry.

"Well Dan and Jim, we decided that we need to have a New York-based vendor in the finalist pool. Besides, you were the only group that included a DVD of your entire proposal including interactive exhibits. Who did this for you?"

"I did." Dan said.

"Very impressive" He said. "We would like to see more of this kind of work at your finalist presentation."

"Got it covered." Dan replied. "Does your conference room have an open wi-fi or internet connection?" He asked.

"I will make sure to have one available. You guys are on for next Monday at three PM. You will have about an hour."

"Works for us." I said.

Dan thanked him and we hung up.

It was a high-five moment.

"This is your presentation Dan." I told him. "Let me know who you want there and what you want them to say."

"We have a week, but I will let you know tomorrow."

We arrived at the meeting a half hour early and a few minutes later the largest vendor and current incumbent came out of the room. I knew one of them and wished them well.

Dan had invited me, the CEO, the Clinical Director and the CIO.

While setting up his laptop, plugging it into the internet connection and tuning up the LCD projector he introduced us and ask the CEO to take five minutes to paint his vision of our company. He did so professionally and flawlessly. Then he turned back to Dan.

Dan flipped on the screen where he had several linked logos for our various departments and capabilities. He turned to the buying group which consisted of ten people representing the ten business and actuarial groups of Empire Blue Cross.

"It doesn't matter where we start here so let me ask you what is your priority." Dan had been well schooled but had taken the consultative sell to a new level.

The Vice President of Group Sales spoke first, "That DVD you sent us was very impressive. Let's hear about your IT department.'

Dan clicked on a link directly to our intranet that pulled up an internal menu and then turned to our CIO and asked her to walk them through the inner workings of our layered servers, remote back-up and web-enabled intuitive software. She then went on with mind-boggling descriptions that none of us on our side of the table could understand. But when she nodded for approval we followed.

After her presentation the VP of Actuary asked about our clinical capabilities.

Dan linked us up again and called on our Clinical Director.

Same scenario.

It was mind-numbingly impressive.

The whole presentation was beyond my scope of understanding. I had cloned myself and he was better.

And frankly, it blew the selection committee out of their chairs.

This was not a sales presentation. It was a statement of confidence, an affirmation of intelligence and a slam-dunk of undeniable competence.

When we didn't win the account I was flabbergasted.

But what happened next was worth it.

It turned out that the incumbent retained the business. But their new contract was conditional on their ability to develop a strategic alliance with us in order to incorporate our technology. Empire Blue Cross wanted our technology, but knew we weren't big enough to handle their business.

At that time we were about one tenth the size of this behemoth competitor. But, here they were, hat in hand, trying to save one of their largest accounts, humbled and embarrassed by the position they were forced to assume.

We invited them over to meet with us.

We knew they were going to have to travel sixty miles up the Jersey turnpike and across one of the bridges to see us. An executive from Capital Blue Cross also came in for the meeting.

It was time to come clean.

Once everyone was in place, including our house counsel and the house counsel from our competitor, our CEO stood to lay it out.

"Great to have you here and I want to introduce you to our CIO."

Our CIO had a yellow pad and she started down a list of questions for our friendly, but enormous, competitor. Fortunately they had brought their CIO also. After-all this was to be a blending of technology.

The questions were designed to point out that our competitor had the same technology we had touted at our sales presentation. We were just better at selling it.

And the stuff they didn't have we weren't willing to share.

Basically we unwound the sale. But we had made an enormous impression in the marketplace and with our biggest competitor.

We became know as the small hi-tech company with the best sales presentation in the New York market.

Dan became one of my most successful sales executives and has subsequently put together a very impressive company of his own.

Turns out that before Dan came to work for us he had worked for Empire Blue Cross in one of their field sales offices. No one at their corporate office knew him. But he had won our opportunity to bid by networking through his old contacts to get us to the table.

Some of you may question as to why all of these stories do not end with an impressive sale. Learning to sell and keep your job in any economy is driven by a number of lessons and techniques. Some are learned through making the sale and some are learned by losing the sale. But they are lessons nevertheless. Here are some that Dan taught me:

1. You can never be too smart or have too many smart people around you

2. Being smart means nothing if you don't know how to show people you are smart

3. Customers buy from companies they perceive to be smarter than other companies.

4. Using contemporary technology does not mean you step away from consultative selling

5. Competitive goliaths can be brought down by agility and intelligence.

Chapter 16

Who Gets to Ask for the Order?

**What is to give light
must endure burning.**
- Victor Frankl, Auschwitz survivor
Author of <u>Man's Search for Meaning</u>

"Hey Bob, this is Jim." I was calling the CEO of a large Ohio-based insurance company.

"That was a great presentation last week." He said. "What can I do for you?"

"Well, Bob." I hesitated, "Just calling to see if you have reached a decision."

This was always a hard question to ask.

"We did right after we met with you. Didn't my VP call you?"

"Nope," I was dying.

He laughed. "You are probably dying. So I won't torture you any more. It was unanimous we are all in. Send us over a contract."

"Dang," I whispered to myself. "This is great. I hope you tell your VP what you put me through."

"Don't worry, I like messing with him."

"Sounds like my boss." I said.

I could have kicked myself for not calling sooner. Only sales people fully understand approach-avoidance psychology. Getting "no" as an answer is painful enough without having to ask for it. So it is natural to avoid it. Honestly this is one of the reasons I gravitated to larger and larger sales. Most of these sales take longer to put together and, frankly, the "no's" come less frequently. When the "no" answer comes they are disappointing. But they are far easier because the sales process has been collaborative and it is not necessary to take the defeat personally.

One of the best "yes's" I received was the for the State of Wyoming Employment system. It was about a ten million dollar account. I had been referred to them by the State of Montana. But like most government business the bidding process was highly regulated and legislated to be transparent.

Flying into Cheyenne, Wyoming is a lot like flying into Tulsa, Oklahoma. Most days are very windy and the other days are like flying into a tornado.

Not really important to the purpose of this story, but most sales executives know that having a white-knuckle flight just before a presentation adds a whole new meaning to "sales anxiety".

I had the enviable position of being the last presenter which had given me a couple of hours to unwind after walking down the stairs from the airplane that was having a hard time staying in place even on the tarmac.

I had gone alone for this presentation. When it was my turn I was told that I could put my slide tray up in the projection room and they handed me a remote to make sure that everything worked. Most of you reading this book are probably wondering how pertinent these sales stories could be if they were from an age before power-points. But I always pushed the envelope with whatever tools were available. Of course the tools only add to the sale, it still takes two or more human beings speaking to each other to close a sale.

For the State of Wyoming my audience was comprised of seven people plus a benefits consultant they had brought in from Denver.

The presentation went off like clockwork and the questions and answers were congenial. When we finished they excused me and I left from the side door of the amphitheater-style lecture room. I walked up the stairs and around to the projection room where I went in to pick up my slide tray.

The committee had obviously forgotten that I needed to get my slide tray and that I could hear their deliberations.

"All in favor of awarding the contract to this last bidder please so indicate."

"They all said 'Yes'."

The Director of Benefits spoke to the rest of the committee. "I am going to run out and see if I can catch Jim before he leaves."

I grabbed my slide tray and ran out of the projection room and started to put on my coat.

"Jim." Bob said. "Glad I caught you. Congratulations, you have won the bid."

"This is great." I said. "But I have a confession."

"What's that?"

"I was in the projection room and heard your vote."

He laughed. "Glad you won. It would have been hard otherwise."

"Bob, you got that right. Can I go down and thank the committee?"

"I was just going to invite you."

When I returned to talk to them Bob told them about me in the projection room. They thought that was pretty funny.

"So" I said. "How did you do this with just a vote? I didn't hear any discussion or deliberation."

Bob turned to the consultant and asked him to answer me.

"After reading your response to our RFP we frankly found your company on a par with the others. But when we started calling references it became apparent that you would carry the day. Frankly, the presentations were necessary for the process but we had already come to a consensus."

"Thank you." I said. "And I guess I better get on the phone and thank those references."

This was a great account and I took Bob on several golf outings to Arizona with my friend from the State of Montana. In many ways I wish the selection committee would have conducted extensive deliberation. It would have been nice to be a fly on the wall.

This is a short chapter but it is imbedded with some important lessons.

1. The larger the sale the less likely you can "ask for the order" at the time of the final presentation. But circling back the next day saves a measurable amount of anxiety.

2. Your best sales are made for you by your current customers

Chapter 17

A Room with a View

**It is not because things are difficult that we do not dare,
it is because we do not dare that they are difficult.**
- Seneca

By their own admission, Marriott Corporation Human Resources Executives admit that their company has become the Ellis Island of the past half century. At any given time they have over a hundred thousand immigrant employees hired as soon as they have their Green Cards. For most of them working for one of the largest companies in America is a springboard to becoming trained workers, learning English and establishing roots in America.

With all of the other business I was doing in the Baltimore/Washington corridor I had wanted to see if it was possible to do business with Marriott.

One afternoon when I was between appointments I decided to drop by and see if I could meet with someone in their Benefits Department.

Strange that I would think this would work. After all, I don't make cold calls on the phone or in person.

As I parked my car in their International Headquarters in Bethesda I thought of the hundreds of other Fortune 500 company home offices that I had entered. Many were quite spectacular. One of the most impressive was John Deere in Moline. They actually brought a babbling brook and meadow indoors with full-size trees and grass. Employees felt like work was a day in the park.

Companies like Eaton Corporation in Cleveland Ohio, Borg Warner in Chicago, Dow Chemical in Midland Michigan, Borden Foods and Nationwide insurance Company both in Columbus, Ohio and other noticeable brands had pretty ordinary home offices. These were clean, impressive, large; but ordinary.

Alcoa Aluminum in Pittsburgh is a contemporary corporate temple.

Other corporate offices were next to and dwarfed by their manufacturing facilities.

Oddly, I worked with a number of small entrepreneurs that helped me broker my products and services that had more palatial offices than those of many corporate CEOs. But the egos of these brokers were the fulcrums on which I was able to leverage the largest accounts.

In addition to Fortune 500 Companies I had also been to places like the CIA where a company I worked for insured their computer installation. Walter Reed Hospital isn't that impressive from the outside, but the historical significance of the Eisenhower wing was a reverent place to be.

When working on the Department of Defense Statement of Work I had the opportunity to attend meetings in the Pentagon.

All of these memories raced through my mind as I walked into the doors of Marriott Headquarters.

"Strange," I thought. "This was the first time that I had ever tried to call on a major corporation…cold."

In some ways it felt like home. For most of my sales career I stayed almost exclusively at Marriott Hotels. In addition to being clean and upscale without being over-the-top, they also have a *killer* frequent traveler program.

I went to the front desk and ask for directions to the Benefits Department.

"Do you have an appointment?" The Security Receptionist was smart and courteous.

"No. But here is my card." I said as I handed her my card.

"One moment please."

She called a number, had a short conversation and then looked up at me.

"Ms. Bingham will be down shortly. Please have a seat." She pointed to some comfortable sofas in a well-appointed area.

Ms. Bingham arrived less than three minutes later. She stopped by the front desk where the clerk gave her my card and pointed to where I was sitting.

As she approached I stood.

"Ms. Bingham?"

"Yes, but you can call me Maureen. How may I help you?"

Interesting how corporate employees are so open and willing to help.

"You can call me Jim. I just want to introduce myself. I have a number of clients in this part of the country and thought I could be helpful to Marriott Corporation."

I opened my brief case and handed her a partial list of clients with names and telephone numbers.

"This is impressive." She said as she looked through the list of about ten of my clients that were within a three-hundred mile radius. "I rarely have people call on me un-announced and when they do they usually want to leave a sales brochure."

She seemed genuinely pleased.

"Frankly," I said. "I have never just stopped by a corporate head-quarters before so I had little to lose."

"I see by your card what business you are in. But I have to admit that I am curious as to your client list. May I make a few calls and then get back to you?"

"Of course," I replied. "Thank you so much for stepping away from your work. May I have one of your cards?"

"Sure." She pulled one out of her day planner and handed it to me.

On the way home I called my office and had my Administrative Assistant drop Ms. Bingham a thank you note that included a list of ten more clients.

"Jim Thompson," I said as I answered my cell phone.

"This is Maureen Bingham at Marriott Corporate." It had only been five days later.

"Hello Maureen. What a coincidence, I am staying in your Lincolnshire Marriott Resort north of Chicago."

"I understand that is one of our nicer properties." She replied.

"Sure is. You have a very nice golf course here and I often invite my Chicago clients to join me at the Dinner Theater here on the property."

"That sounds great." She was definitely pleased. "I have made some calls, both to the references you left and to the ones you had forwarded to me. When are you going to be back on the East Coast? I would like to explore some possibilities with you."

We made an appointment and started a several month process of plan designs and discussions with the several divisions of Marriott Corporation. It was not without its challenges, but Maureen became an internal coach and advocate. Turns out she introduced me to other decision makers the same way I introduced myself to her. She simply passed on my client list.

Like most others, they invited in some competitors to validate our proposal, but Marriott become a long and loyal account.

I had very few other opportunities to call on corporate accounts unannounced. And those where I tried were typically met with multi-levels of gate-keepers. But I usually left a short client list and my business card. I also found that when approaching a new client by mail, a client reference list was far more successful than enclosing a sales brochure.

The sales strategies here are obvious but worth listing:

1. Personal cold calls on prospects may get you more than a soft seat in a big lobby

2. Always carry copies of a good client reference list with you

3. If you do not have a good client reference list, stop selling immediately and spend more time with your current clients

4. Know where your prospects are located, just for when you are in the neighborhood

5. Call on people from whom you buy products and services

Chapter 18

Third Party Perks

**I believe that having something new happen,
no matter how small,
is what makes for a healthy day,
no matter how many days may be left.**
- *David Greenberger, from his essay As I Grow Old,
included in the essay collection,
This I Believe II: More Personal Philosophies of Remarkable Men and Women*

Many industries and potential prospects are accessible through little-known layers of other companies or organizations. These third parties sometimes control the decision process hidden far away from the front door of the main office.

In most industries there are coalitions, supply chains, affinity groups, buying groups and trade organizations.

One of the markets where I have enjoyed considerable success is Third Party Administrators (TPAs). These are organizations that process and pay health-care claims for organizations that self-insure their employees or members. There are several thousand TPAs in the country and most of them work with employers that have from fifty to ten thousand employees. Larger groups are almost always self-insured, but they use Blue Cross or other large insurance companies to process their claims for them.

TPAs will have from five to over a hundred separate companies as clients and aggregate purchasing for them of all insurance-related products. These products include hospital networks with negotiated discounts, vision, dental and prescription plans as well as group life insurance, 401-K plans, retirement plans and many others.

TPA owners are typically very entrepreneurial and are constantly on the hunt for more products and services for their clients.

Over my career I worked with hundreds of TPAs. In some cases I would win their whole book of business and in others I would be one of a select few of preferred vendors.

One of my TPA clients located in Peoria, Illinois approached me with an interesting proposal. I was in his office at the time meeting with his VP of Operations. He came up to me after the meeting.

"Are you flying back to Chicago this afternoon?" He asked.

"Sure am. I've got a couple of meetings there tomorrow then on to Detroit for the rest of the week."

"I am heading to Chicago too." He said. "I am leaving in about an hour. How would you like to fly up with me in my new corporate jet?"

This was my first invite to ride in a corporate jet. Funny it should be out of Peoria. But there had been other nice surprises in Peoria. When I had first started to work with this TPA they had recommended that I stay in Jummer's Hotel. It is a medieval-looking place with a fabulous German restaurant. After the first time I was hooked and stayed there every time I was in Peoria.

An hour later we were boarding his private jet with a couple of other execs. Once we had reached altitude he leaned over from his huge leather, reclining seat and said. "Take a look at this."

He pulled a brief case out from the side of his seat and placed it on the table in front of him. He snapped it open and lifted the top.

"Ever seen a satellite phone?" he asked.

I hadn't, except in Sharper Image catalogues.

It was very old-school compared to the cell phones of today. But it was 1988. It was the stuff of Maxwell Smart.

"Go ahead," he said as he handed me the handset. "Give your wife a call."

"You are kidding?" I asked.

He just nodded and I dialed.

It was cool. Very, very cool.

Being in sales is not without perks and this was one of thousands that I have enjoyed.

After we finished playing with his new toy he turned to me, "I've just been appointed to the National Board for the B'nai B'rith Auxiliary. Do you have any idea what that is?" he asked.

"Not exactly, but I would guess it is the Jewish organization?" I asked.

"Correct." He affirmed.

"They have asked me to put together a discount health care plan for them for our members that do not have health insurance. But I need help with a drug plan."

Did I mention that working with in sales has its perks?

The next week we were together again. This time at the B'nai B'rith Auxiliary headquarters in Washington DC. My friend in Peoria had already vouched for me and my company, he had told me what kind of plan they needed and I had prepared an "educational presentation". No need to try to sell anything. These people just needed to know how the plan could work for them. My client from Peoria had already made the sale for me.

Like most similar presentation I made sure that there was audience interaction. But one of the Board Members hadn't said anything. Finally, at the end of the meeting he indicated he had a question.

"This has been very interesting. But let me ask this one question. Why would anyone want to have their prescriptions mailed to them? We have always just had our maid pick up our prescriptions when she does our grocery shopping."

Sometimes even highly intelligent customers remain clueless. I was stunned at his insulation from the real world. Sure, part of our presentation was to assure people that all prescriptions needed for immediate use, antibiotics and first time therapeutics should best be purchased at a local pharmacy. But assuming that everyone had a maid to do this for them was beyond belief.

Fortunately my TPA client looked over at this board member and said, "Herb, do you really think that every member of the B'nai B'rith has a maid?"

This brought a laugh from the rest of the group and we closed the deal.

But it was a "better-than-sweet" win.

In order to meet the specific needs of this group, they wanted my firm to provide actuarial funding.

My company was not willing to do this. But undeterred I asked them if I could take the deal outside of our company. We would still provide the mail-service prescription dispensing and delivery, but I would need to come up with a strategic partner.

I called my friend back in Peoria and asked him if he would like to go into business with me.

We put together an LLC, subcontracted with the company I worked for and packaged a multi-million dollar sale.

A year later the program was doing very well so I went back to my Peoria partner and asked him if I could buy him out.

He bought me out instead.

Did I say that sales has perks?

These sales techniques are easy to teach others:

1. Find the middle-men in your industry

2. Turn the middle-men into customers and then into brokers of your services

3. The perks of your customers can be your tools

4. If your company cannot handle the business then start your own business

Chapter 19

Play for Success

The secret of happiness is curiosity.
- Norman Douglas, author

I called the Camelback Marriott Resort in Scottsdale. "What is your corporate room rate per night for a weekend in August?" I asked.

"Thank you for calling the Camelback Marriott Resort and let me check that for you." The clerk was precise and courteous.

"That will be eighty-seven dollars plus tax." He replied.

"Do you have a golf package?" I asked. "I have played your golf course and would like to bring in some clients."

"Yes sir. Let me check that for you."

I heard the keyboard clattering.

"Sir, our golf package includes our deluxe room with king size bed, a complimentary breakfast, a bucket of balls at our driving range and eighteen holes of golf including greens fees and cart. The price is eighty-five dollars plus tax."

I let it sink in for a minute.

"But that is two dollars less than the regular room rate." I replied.

"Yes sir. As you know, temperatures in August are usually over a hundred and ten so we like to provide an incentive for our customers to play our golf course."

Sounds fun.

So for the next three Augusts I took some of my largest customers to Scottsdale to play golf. And on the cheap!

By this time in my career I had negotiated myself out of a corporate position and was working as an independent contractor on pure commission. It was worth it and I even covered my own expenses. Getting paid directly for my results and re-investing in my client-relationships gave me the freedom to brand the company I represented and to brand myself.

We would fly in on Thursday afternoon and play golf at Mountain Shadows Executive course. Rated as one of the top ten short courses in the country it was a great way to get started (and lose most of the new balls I gave them in the ponds and creeks that ran through the course.) August evenings in Scottsdale are beautiful but still over a hundred and ten degrees.

The next morning we would tee off at the Camelback course at six am while it was still cool (only about a hundred). Then we would hang out at the pool the rest of the day before playing an evening eighteen at another course.

Saturday morning we would hit one of the new premier courses in the area. Then back to the pool and then out for a great dinner at one of the local restaurants. One year we also caught an NFL pre-season game.

Sunday morning we would usually play a course in Phoenix or Tempe on the way to the airport.

These clients loved the outings and the heat was the constant joke.

I have been playing golf with clients for over three decades. I rarely break ninety but neither do my clients. I can't play well enough to let them win. So that is never a part of our game. I have never belonged to a private country club, mostly because I wasn't home enough to make it worthwhile. But I have been a guest of many clients at their private clubs.

I rank golf as the second best way to entertain clients. It is engaging enough to be interesting, but loose enough to allow for conversation.

Most important, golf allows you the opportunity to show your client that you have honesty and integrity. No one likes a cheat. And no one will do business with a cheat. No matter how bad I played I always took the full number of strokes. If a client insisted that I take a mulligan I would. But that would be tempered with asking him to clarify any rules I had a question about. And I always asked him (or her) to drive the cart.

Walking a course with a client never worked for me. If we couldn't ride in a cart together the whole point was missed. Even if no business is discussed the strategy is to learn about each other. I only had one client that insisted on walking the course. But it was a private course that required that we walk and have caddies. I tried to keep my shots as close to his as possible in order to walk and talk together.

Granted, not all clients play golf and there are seasons of the year when it is impossible. But I have gone fishing, boating, sailing, attended sports events, went to Broadway shows and done hundreds of other things with clients.

One of my good friends was the corporate sales "host" for one of the large oil companies. We attended the same church and each Sunday I would ask him what he had done the week before.

It was almost as much fun to hear about his trips as it might have been to go with him. He would go Pariah fishing in the Amazon, grouse hunting in Mexico, whale watching off the coast of California, wild boar hunting in Russia, mountain climbing on Kilimanjaro, safaris to African, Penguin watching at the South Pole, and exploring the islands of the Philippines.

Have you noticed that no matter what you do, or have done, there is always something more out there?

In my opinion lunches and dinners are the best venues for entertainment. I say this selfishly because when traveling on business I hate to eat alone. So I book my lunches and dinners first and then fill in the rest.

But there are some interesting conclusions I have reached about dining with clients and prospects. Mostly they are observations, not rules or suggestions. Just observations.

I don't drink.

When I first entered corporate life one of my bosses told me that I would never succeed in corporate life unless I started to drink.

I guess I could have been more successful. But I discovered that once people knew I didn't drink they made sure I didn't feel uncomfortable for not drinking. This continues to be a unique position for me.

And historically I have witnessed a number of changes in this regard.

In the late seventies to early eighties it was common for people to have martinis at lunch. I once worked with a man who had several at lunch and came back to work frequently suggesting that one or more of us take the rest of the day off. We knew better, but there were days when it was tempting.

Through the eighties and nineties martini lunches evolved into "glass of wine" lunches and then they evolved into "mineral or sparkling water" lunches. Perrier and Pellegrino became the common favorites.

Over the past decade my clients usually ask for a diet soda or water.

Wine with dinner has continued to be a constant unless it is a "beer" place. But again I have never felt left out and my clients never felt uncomfortable.

I might add that in some ways I envy my peers who drink wine and know how to "talk" wine. I am sure they have been able to relate to clients and make sales that I missed. But I guess it is an acquired taste and an acquired skill.

But there is a point here. We each have unique strengths and experiences. We cannot be everything to everyone. I love people but I know I am far more effective at a dinner than at a cocktail party.

It goes without saying that when entertaining at a restaurant asking your client where they would most like to eat is always the best strategy, particularly if you are not in your home town. But even then it should be their preference as to type of food.

During most of my career I lived in a suburb of Philadelphia. I dined at most of the places in and around the city. But just like with friends, everyone has their preferences and sometimes a client would surprise me and say they would love to get a cheese-steak at Pat's or Gino's in South Philly rather than have a French Cuisine at Le Bec Fin.

How, and when, to conduct business while dining also has to be at the pleasure of the client. There is a wonderful sub-level Spanish restaurant in Baltimore called Tio Pepe's on Franklin Street. This is a great change in a city otherwise known for its blue claw crabs and other sumptuous seafood. But at Tio Pepe's you can get a private room to discuss the most confidential of business deals...or not!

It is a temptation to provide a "restaurant guide" for every city where I have conducted business in the country. But the point is that business is conducted over food in almost every sales environment.

For several years I was a member-guest at the prestigious Union League Club in Philadelphia.

At the time it was just as all-white-male-stodgy as the name and building implied. But, in its day, in corporate circles in Philadelphia, it was the place to see and be seen.

To pay or not to pay?

I paid ninety percent of the time.

The exceptions were when invited by clients to their private clubs where guests were not allowed to pay. An example of this is The Vanguard Group, the investment and mutual funds home office located in Malvern, Pennsylvania. They have a strict entertainment policy which precludes their corporate staff from leaving the premises on business lunches and so we ate in their corporate cafeteria. But even in their cafeteria they were not allowed to have vendors pay for their lunch. They also were not allowed to pay for me.

I have also attended lunches with top corporate executives who had "private" lunch facilities just for the top tier executives. These small dining rooms were all crystal and starched linen. And again there was no money exchanged. It was a perk that they were happy to share.

A very successful strategy that I used was to offer to have lunches catered-in when I was invited to meet with groups of five to twenty-five people. On those occasions I would ask the buyer's administrative Assistant to order from their favorite caterer and I would cover the bill. These working lunches were appreciated by busy departments and executives who otherwise may not have had time to meet with me.

So the opportunities are endless and rarely disappoint. But there are some techniques to be learned.

1. Whether it is golf, tennis or other competitive sports, no matter your skill level; know the rules and etiquette of play and never cheat.

2. As with all other tools, make sure to listen to what your client's interests are before bull-dogging them into attending a Rodeo. (Big challenge for me because I love Rodeos.)

3. Know your client's tolerance levels for alcohol. This is driven by not only their personal mores, but the customs of the geographic area where you are doing business.

4. When dining for entertainment, give your client the choice. Not just as a part of their personal preference for the food, but also being respectful of their time restraints and the type of ambiance they prefer at the time.

Chapter Twenty

SALES
in Your Life?

**The willow knows what the storm does not:
that the power to endure harm
outlives the power to inflict it.**
- Blood of the Martyr

Child Protective Services is not the only vocation in which a good friend of mine excels. She also prepares taxes for clients whose first language is Spanish. She is bi-lingual and though she had been raised in a middle-class neighborhood of Orange County California she works in the hidden barrios tucked away in unrecognized corners of the Southern California from Anaheim to Encinitas.

The names of the places are not important, and even the names of her clients all run together as an alphabet soup of Hispanic monikers.

What is important is the "sales" she makes every day. She handles from five to fifteen child protective services cases per week.

Recently she found a five year old little boy that was so plagued by scabies and epidermal dysplasia that the skin over his entire body had the texture of an elephant. He had lost all of the hair from the top of his head and the tips of his fingers and toes were inflamed and painful to touch. He had open sores all over his body.

She found him in a home with a mother and five other children. There was little to eat and what assistance money the mother had received she had been using for drugs. All of the children were in need of medical attention,' food and clothing but the little boy was in the worst condition. With the help of a local police officer she took the children to Orangewood Children's Home and then the little boy to Children's Hospital.

And then the work began. Finding other family members from as far away as San Francisco to come and take the children and the little boy.

Some two months ago on Christmas Eve she had been called into a child abuse situation and there she found little seven week old Nathan, dead from brain hemorrhage...shaken baby syndrome. On Christmas Eve she had a "sale" to make. Find a home for his three siblings and work with the police to find and arrest an abusive father.

Both of these little boys suffered these tragic circumstances within the shadows of Disneyland.

Her daily "sales" objectives over-shadows anything I have ever sold.

One of my closest friends left corporate life a little less than a decade ago and went into academia where she has been teaching graduate-level business courses to adults.

She typically begins her classes by asking her students why they have decided at mid-career to extend their education. The answers are varied. But mostly they think an MBA will move them to the next level: to get a raise, a promotion or a better job.

Her "sales" challenge is to convince them that an additional acronym after their name or on their resume` is worth no more than their ability to step into their existing career with renewed commitment, enthusiasm, networking skills, and to let their voice be heard above the rest. She has written a book to help them and anyone else looking to further their careers entitled "Brown-Nosing 101". It is a guide to formulating your own "stimulus- bailout".

I have a life-long friend who is President of a Public Broadcasting Station (PBS) in California. His station, like all other PBS stations is reliant on the generosity of donors, both big and small. Today's economy has hit them very hard. Pledges from working people have all but dried up. Pledges from corporate and wealthy donors have been slashed dramatically. Their normal telethon pledge month has been extended indefinitely.

He has some "sales" challenges to meet.

So as in these cases, and a myriad of similar situations "sales" go far beyond the confines of traditional "sales" jobs. "You can be a social worker, a college professor, in public broadcasting or even just a home-owner trying to convince your bank or a different bank to work with you on keeping your home.

And then, like my brother who is a highly skilled automotive engineer, there are hundreds of thousands of you who are looking for a job.

Of course finding a job, any job, is a "big sale". Even a job paying forty-thousand dollars a year with normal inflation bumps is worth close to half a million dollars over the next decade, and that does not include most benefit packages that are worth at least ten thousand dollars a year.

As a result of discussing "Learning to Sell and Stay Employed" with people from many walks of life the response is that techniques offered in this book can be universally applied.

As a conclusion to the experiences in this book and those that you may have remembered while reading it I propose the following:

1. Learning to sell is relative to the importance of the situation not the size of the revenue or commission.

2. Selling crosses all human transactions

3. Sales techniques can be used by people of all ages in all circumstances

4. Learning sales techniques will change your life

5. These hundred sales techniques are not all of them

Prologue

Success doesn't come to you…you go to it.
- Marva Collins, educator

It had just turned dark on an early November snowy evening and I had a hundred miles to drive before reaching Helena, Montana. I had made several trips before, but this time I had decided to take a more scenic route that appeared to be shorter. It was a fifty-mile canyon road. Within ten miles of heading up the canyon I was engulfed in a winter snow white-out. Visibility was less than twenty feet and it was difficult to discern where the road surface stopped and where the wildly whipping snow began. To further exacerbate my situation I could not see more than a foot or two out my side windows, yet I knew that along many stretches there were severe cliffs.

As I proceeded slowly, knowing that turning back was no option and stopping may doom me as an unsuspecting target for other traffic, I noticed a reflection ahead. As I approached I saw that it was a road-side reflection pole, an eight-foot metal pole, with a reflector on top.

But, as I passed this reflector I was unable to see the next one. For at least fifty yards I was left to crawl along, hoping not to slide off the cliff or into an embankment. But then, just as I was about to give up hope the next reflector appeared. I adjusted my driving accordingly. So I went; one reflector to the next with no direction in between.

For me this BIG SALE was to convince myself that I could just keep moving forward.

And I did.

What You Paid for
Without Reading the Book

Over 100 Sales Techniques
No Matter What Your Field

1. Unsolicited business should be humanized as soon as possible.

2. Get in front of the buyer(s).

3. Once in front of your buyer(s) try your best to listen to why they are buying. For good salesmen this is very difficult. For great salesmen it is imperative.

4. Introduce up-line management as soon as possible through a positive introduction. If you do not believe in or trust your boss, sell for somebody else. No matter what the product buyers must be given the opportunity to believe that it is you and the company that stand behind your promises.

5. Return their phone calls by the end of the day (their time).

6. If you do not know the answers to their questions, tell them immediately. No hesitation, no vacillation no equivocation.

7. When you are brought in as the "boss" allow your sales executive to take the lead. Respect the surgeon.

8. When confronted with new obstacles ask the client to help you solve the problem.

9. Involve the potential buyer in writing the contract.

10. In a highly political environment recognize that the "spin" is up to the client.

11. Do not dwell on personal issues or exploit tragedies with your prospects. But do not discount them either.

12. Never underestimate your own ambition

13. Product knowledge is important but not as important as you may think.

14. Strategic "Influence Marketing" is always worth dividing up the profits!

15. Enjoy the sales process and your clients will enjoy buying from you

16. Make friends along the way. They always pay off.

17. Dark suits, white or light shirts, conservative ties. Dress like the President of the United States or if a woman like TV anchorwomen. CNN, Fox or CNBC are excellent choices. If that is too lofty for you, and you only sell in your state, Google your Senators and dress like they do.

18. Understated exudes confidence

19. Clean is mandatory. Hands, hair, face and shoes. Polished shoes are never old-fashion. Carry one of those quick-polish pads in your brief-case. And don't hesitate to hit your brief-case with it either.

20. Dress for the culture and for the event.

21. Let your customers know that you have a broad choice of products or solutions, but try to limit the best choices for their situation.

22. Most customers choose the same thing, but let them come to that conclusion on their own.

23. Up-selling only works if you try it.

24. Know the demographics of your marketplace and play to them with indigenous strategies

25. Be ready for cultural anomalies. By the end of the day we all have the same motivations, needs and emotions.

26. Sometimes good things happen under the worst of circumstances.

27. Innovation works but requires collaboration

28. Co-branding-by-association embracing contemporary trends can be defining

29. Stepping out of industry mores with proper branding supersedes pricing competition

30. Extraordinary Service is priceless, but you need to "sell it"

31. Take every opportunity to learn everything you can about your company and its products and services.

32. Writing well helps you sell well.

33. Your work can always be improved

34. Sweating at work is what they pay you for.

35. Working for an SOB can help you prevent being one yourself

36. Always show up with your guns loaded

37. Keep the safety on

38. Be prepared for someone else to be the buyer

39. When you ask, be prepared to listen

40. Selling is sometimes done by the buyer

41. Sometimes a loss is a win

42. Your ability to converse intelligently is in direct proportion to your life's experiences.

43. Your success in sales is directly proportional to things you find in common with your clients.

44. Selling anything helps you sell everything.

45. You have the possibility of making more sales while doing something you have in common with your client outside their office.

46. Most of your sales will happen because you love to sell and your customer loves to buy.

47. Beyond jokes and stories, if you are having fun in your life it will show in your career.

48. Never underestimate the capacity of your mind and your body.

49. Faith is universal.

50. No matter what your age, it is never too late to expand your life experiences.

51. Every target market has an opening

52. If you aren't the person to make the sale, bring in the person who will

53. Make your customers your brain trust

54. Do not be afraid to repeat success

55. Sharing the sales process means you have people to celebrate with.

56. Selling is always collaborative

57. Sex sells.

58. Skill always trumps race

59. If you are a man, get over it

60. Get the right person for the job.

61. Always let your family and friends know what you sell and why you sell it.

62. Never underestimate the help of family and friends. They may be in places you could never go on your own.

63. Where you came from is who you are and most people came from similar places. Let them know.

64. Know when to use your boss and when not to.

65. Even Four Star Generals buy things

66. If you have ever learned anything, you can learn more

67. Refuse to be intimidated by your ignorance

68. Know when you don't know something and bring in the experts

69. Do not underestimate what your client does not know

70. At some point in the sales process make sure that your client hears all of your company's capabilities

71. Never underestimate the ambition of your salespeople

72. Hiring experienced sales people has two advantages: what they can do and what they can do for you.

73. Good telemarketers are worth every penny you pay them.

74. Being good at what you do is not necessarily appreciated by everyone.

75. Get to know your industry's trade groups and invite yourself to speak to them

76. You can never be too smart or have too many smart people around you

77. Being smart means nothing if you don't know how to show people you are smart

78. Customers buy from companies they perceive to be smarter than other companies.

79. Using contemporary technology does not mean you step away from consultative selling

80. Competitive goliaths can be brought down by agility and intelligence.

81. The bigger the sale the less likely the opportunity to "ask for the order" at the time of the final presentation. But circling back the next day saves a measurable amount of anxiety.

82. Your best sales are made for you by your current customers

83. Personal cold calls on prospects may get you more than a soft seat in a big lobby

84. Always carry copies of a good client reference list with you

85. If you do not have a good client reference list, stop selling immediately and spend more time with your current clients

86. Know where your prospects are located, just for when you are in the neighborhood

87. Call on people who you buy products and services from

88. Find the middle-men in your industry.

89. Turn the middle-men into customers and then into brokers of your services.

90. The perks of your customers can be your tools.

91. If your company cannot handle the business then start your own business.

92. Whether it is golf, tennis or other competitive sports, no matter your skill level; know the rules and etiquette of play and never cheat.

93. As with all other tools, make sure to listen to what your client's interests are before bull-dogging them into attending a Rodeo.

94. Know your client's tolerance levels for alcohol. This is driven by not only their personal mores, but the customs of the geographic area where you are doing business.

95. When dining for entertainment, give your client the choice. Not just as a part of their personal preference for the food, but also being respectful of their time restraints and the type of ambiance they prefer at the time.

96. Learning to sell is relative to the importance of the situation not the size of the revenue or commission.

97. Selling crosses all human transactions

98. Sales techniques can be used by people of all ages in all circumstances.

99. Learning sales techniques will change your life.

100. These hundred sales techniques are not all of them.

And from great minds come even greater ideas

**The way to love anything
is to realize that it might be lost.**
- *G.K. Chesterton, author*

My life is my message.
- *Mahatma Gandhi*

Always do what you are afraid to do.
- *Ralph Waldo Emerson*

A man is about as big as the things that make him angry.
- *Winston Churchill*

**Look within, for within is the wellspring of virtue,
which will not cease flowing, if you cease not from digging.**
- *Marcus Aurelius*

**Tolerance implies no lack of commitment to one's own beliefs.
Rather it condemns the oppression or persecution of others.**
- *John F. Kennedy*

If the world seems cold to you, kindle fires to warm it.
- *Lucy Larcom, poet*

**If you don't learn from your mistakes,
there's no sense making them.**
- *Anonymous*

The question should be,
is it worth trying to do,
not can it be done.
- Allard Lowenstein, American diplomat

The willow knows what the storm does not:
that the power to endure harm outlives the power to inflict it.
- Blood of the Martyr

It is not because things are difficult that we do not dare,
it is because we do not dare that they are difficult.
- Seneca

I don't believe people are looking for the meaning of life
as much as looking for the experience of being alive.
- Joseph Campbell, author of the classic The Power of Myth.

Great spirits have always encountered violent opposition
from mediocre minds.
- Albert Einstein

To dare is to lose one's footing momentarily.
To not dare is to lose oneself.
- Soren Kierkegaard, Philosopher and Theologian

What is to give light must endure burning.
- Victor Frankl, Auschwitz survivor
author of the must-read classic, Man's Search for Meaning.

Think of all the beauty still left around you and be happy.
- Anne Frank

To love and win is the best thing.
To love and lose, the next best.
- William M. Thackeray, novelist

All the joy the world contains
Has come through wishing happiness for others.
All the misery the world contains
Has come through wanting pleasure for oneself.
- Indian philosopher-poet Shantideva

The world is a dangerous place,
not because of those who do evil,
but because of those who look on and do nothing.
- Albert Einstein

The real joy of life is in its play.
Play is anything we do for the joy and love of doing it,
apart from any profit, compulsion, or sense of duty.
It is the real joy of living.
- Walter Rauschbusch, theologian

When one door closes another door opens;
but we often look so long and so regretfully upon the closed door,
that we do not see the ones which open for us.
- Alexander Graham Bell

Life's most persistent and urgent question is,
'What are you doing for others?'"
- Martin Luther King

I believe that having something new happen,
no matter how small,
is what makes for a healthy day,
no matter how many days may be left.
- *David Greenberger, from his essay As I Grow Old,
included in the essay collection, This I Believe II: More Personal Philosophies of Remarkable Men and Women.*

The only normal people
are the ones you don't know very well.
- *Joe Ancis, comedian*

Being defeated is often only a temporary condition.
Giving up is what makes it permanent.
- *Marilyn vos Savant, columnist and very smart person*

I am always doing that which I cannot
in order that I may learn how to do it.
- *Pablo Picasso*

The secret of happiness is curiosity.
- *Norman Douglas, author*

You were born an original.
Don't die a copy.
- *John Mason, author*

Success doesn't come to you…you go to it.
- *Marva Collins, educator*

About the Author

James R. Thompson has spent more than three decades selling to a broad variety of clients including Fortune 1,000 companies, unions, cities, States, the Federal Government, insurances companies, the military and anyone that would buy an ice cream cone. He currently lives in a high mountain resort in Utah where he skis, trains horses, motorcycles, offers consulting services, sales training and writes. "Learn to Sell and Stay Employed in Any Economy" is his third book.

Other Books by James R. Thompson

A View From Within an Elephant's Ear, Two Minute Stories of Observation, Reflection, Inspiration and Humor, Granite Publishing 1997

Mormon Cowboy, Real Cowboy Stories! Filled with humor, wisdom, adventure, and western lore! iUniverse Publishing 2004